MW01129623

Shared Reading

GRADES 3 AND BEYOND

Working it out together

Sue Brown

 Learning Media®

Acknowledgments

This book and the video that accompanies it are the result of extensive consultation and collaboration. I would like to thank the many people in the United States, Australia, and New Zealand whose contributions have made this project possible.

For direct contributions to the text: Fiona Gilmore, Ro Griffiths, Trevor McDonald, Kathleen McDonnell, and Michelle Wright.

For reviewing the text as it developed: Lyn Bareta, Murray Gadd, Toni Hollingsworth, Michelle Kelly, Libby Limbrick, Lyn Reggett, Diane Snowball, Lois Thompson, Maria Utevsky, Melanie Winthrop, and Susan Young.

For generous and gracious advice, support, and assistance: Brenda Parkes, Susan Cossaboom, Rosemary Fullerton-Smith, Liz Saplin, Margaret Smith, Trish Stevenson, and the many others who have assisted me in schools and with the publishing process.

For your willingness to let me observe your teaching, discuss practice with you, quote from your classroom lessons, and in some cases, record you on video: Suzanne Begovich, Devi Howat, Kathleen Flynn, Cherie Kaplan, Sandi McCallum, Elizabeth Rodriguez, Sue Simpson, Sara Stone, and Rachel Thomas. Thanks also to the other teachers and principals who allowed me to spend time in their classrooms in the formative stages of this project. Your expertise has been a valuable contribution to the content of this book.

Thanks to the students whose words or written work appear in the text.

To the team at Learning Media who helped bring it all together, my most sincere thanks: Valerie Anderson, Jeannie Beauchamp, Kelvin Cunningham (designer), Ali Everts (project manager), Simon Minto (editor), and Nicole Wright.

Contents

Introduction

The stage was set. Sara's class gathered expectantly around the screen – the poem was ready to be shared. Sara primed her audience by asking them to pay attention to the images that came to mind as she read. Keeping the title hidden to generate suspense and curiosity, she revealed the text line by line on the overhead. The students leaned forward in rapt silence, following every word with their eyes as Sara evoked the drama and tension of the poem through her expressive reading. When she reached the end of the poem, she simply paused, letting the anticipation swirl around them.

"Get your images ready by describing them in your head the way a writer would," Sara prompted, giving even the quietest student a chance to have words ready.

"Now turn to a neighbor and share your ideas about the poem. Tell your neighbor about the images you had and the words that described these images."

> **Twister**
>
> Sinister magician
> you make things
> disappear.
> Houses, trees –
> their roots conjured up
> from the ground.
>
> Even at sea
> you strike.
> Tall waterspout
> like a sea serpent
> snaking its way
> across the waves.
>
> Jenny Bornholdt, 2004

The conversation was intense as students shared and justified their assertions about the poem and its possible subject. After a few minutes, Sara redirected their attention to the poem, reading it again as they followed with their eyes. She called on three or four students to share the discussions they'd had. Eventually, she uncovered the title and probed for more depth and detail from her students:

- *How does the writer feel about the twister? What words tell you this?*
- *What is she comparing it to? Why is this effective?*
- *How could she know about twisters?*

Sara had three objectives for this lesson: she wanted her students to experience and enjoy a well-written poem; she wanted them to think about the writer's sources of information; and she wanted them to identify the ways in which the writer conveyed her feelings about tornadoes. In exploring sources of information and ways of conveying feelings, Sara drew on her knowledge of her students as writers. She knew they could write good nonfiction using multiple sources of information, but she wanted to show them that the use of the poetic form enabled a writer to convey both factual information and a personal response.

This shared reading lesson engaged a whole class in an enjoyable, instructive experience. By using an enlarged text, the teacher was able to expose the students to the written as well as the spoken words of the poem. The focused questions and the discussion that followed took the students deeper into the meaning of the poem and gave them opportunities to learn more about forms of writing that they could apply in their own reading and writing.

Shared reading gives students the key to the kingdom. Particularly in the upper grades, it's very important for all students in terms of participation and learning. The teacher facilitates the students' internalizing and applying reading strategies that they can use throughout their day and throughout their lives.

Elizabeth, grade 5 teacher

As students move into the intermediate and middle grades, their teachers make assumptions about their ability to read and comprehend texts. The texts that these students encounter are increasingly diverse and complex. Many students make this progression without any trouble. Others need support and explicit instruction to ensure that they don't lose interest or confidence in reading. Shared reading enables teachers to show their students how to read, comprehend, and access information from increasingly sophisticated or unfamiliar texts within a supportive and interactive environment.

In shared reading, students are encouraged to work with the teacher and each other as they develop and master new strategies for making meaning from texts. Successful readers apply many strategies at once and understand that reading is a problem-solving process that requires constant, active engagement with the text. The support available in shared reading helps to make this complex multitasking more visible to students. By being shown how expert readers work, students begin to see how they can apply strategies and problem-solving techniques in their own reading. Because shared reading focuses on working it out together, this approach is a powerful way to build confidence and knowledge as students develop higher-order thinking skills and learn new ways of working with texts.

Who should use this book?

This book explores the use of shared reading with students in grade 3 and beyond, taking into account their changing needs as learners. It's written for teachers of all areas of the curriculum who want to use the approach to develop the reading and writing abilities and critical thinking of their students.

This book is for any teacher who wants to instill a sense of excitement about reading and motivate their students to want to read more. They will find that shared reading is a fresh approach that requires them to share their own passion for reading, their own strategies for making meaning, and their own ways of dealing with novel and unfamiliar texts and topics.

Teachers who are new to the classroom or who are new to this approach will find the support they need to implement shared reading. Literacy coaches, staff developers, and others with a responsibility for improving teaching will find material with which to plan and support professional development.

Teachers who operate programs that use small-group work and individual assignments more than whole-class or large-group instruction will find shared reading valuable as a way to model and develop specific literacy skills and promote discourse in the classroom environment. It can also be used to introduce or review the learning in literature circles, cooperative learning groups, reciprocal teaching, and other student-led activities.

Teachers who mostly use whole-class instruction will learn that shared reading provides a valuable alternative teaching approach that allows more student involvement and increased learning opportunities. It can be used to help the transition from a prescriptive instructional program to a more literature-based, comprehensive, and interactive literacy program.

Teachers of content area subjects such as social studies and science can also use shared reading. It's a highly effective approach to use across the curriculum because it blends subject-specific instruction with teaching the reading and comprehension strategies that students need to access complex texts.

Throughout the book, examples of shared reading texts, teaching suggestions, and extracts from authentic shared reading lessons are used to illustrate and clarify the text.

CHAPTER 1

A Rationale for Shared Reading

An active approach to learning

A great deal of teaching and learning happens every time active learners meet with a responsive teacher to read and reread shared books and to engage in discussion and analysis of texts. With ongoing assessment and the goals of the classroom literacy program in mind, teachers implicitly and explicitly model reading and writing behaviors, skills, and strategies.

Parkes, 2000, page 25

Shared reading is an approach to teaching reading in which a teacher and a group of students come together to read, discuss, and learn from and about texts. It's an approach that allows students to experience the joy of reading, the richness and variety of language, and the stimulation of sharing ideas and information with their peers. As with any act of reading, the prime objective is to make meaning of the text. In shared reading, the teacher stretches learning by showing how expert readers handle texts. The teacher achieves this through implicit and explicit instruction and through quality interactions. In this approach, teachers build on their students' knowledge to help them to deepen their thinking, critically evaluate texts, and become metacognitive readers.

The essential features of shared reading can be listed as follows:

- All eyes are on the same text.

- The teacher (or other expert reader) reads aloud while others follow along silently or join in.

- All students are supported in accessing the text and its meaning.

- The teacher selects the purpose to meet the specific learning needs of the group.

- The teacher chooses the text to match the purpose.

- The text contains an appropriate mix of supports and challenges.

- The teacher and the students engage in discussion to work out meaning together.

As well as these features, shared reading supports the learning of comprehension strategies and information skills across a wide variety of text types. It teaches students skills and strategies that are useful beyond simply understanding the focus text. The reading is an enjoyable, collaborative experience for all participants.

Shared reading has evolved from research carried out several decades ago into the early literacy practices of young children in the home (see, for example,

Holdaway, 1979; Parkes, 2000). Holdaway's research led him to experiment with the reading practices in school that emulated aspects of early home reading. He initially called this "shared-book experience." He and his fellow teachers used enlarged versions of popular stories and poems in intimate settings that allowed the teacher and the students to read aloud together and to participate in enjoyable, stimulating reading experiences.

Brenda Parkes (*Read It Again!*, 2000) encourages teachers to use shared reading in ways that replicate the characteristics that have made the bedtime story such a powerful precursor to successful reading for young children. By doing this, teachers can provide a supportive setting for implicit and explicit teaching with a variety of text types and with active, involved learners.

Characteristics of successful reading experiences for young children include the enjoyable nature of the experience, active participation that increases over time, the collaborative negotiation of meaning, the connections that children are encouraged to make, and the encouragement for children to "internalize process and content" (Parkes, 2000, page 13).

These features can be replicated in school as students move through the reading process and develop their own reading lives. This is why shared reading is an effective approach to teaching reading at all levels of schooling. It reflects a natural learning process that begins early on in our reading lives. Although it looks different with older students, it is based on the same underlying beliefs and theoretical principles.

What distinguishes shared reading from other teaching approaches or practices
is the amount and nature of teacher support for the reading. Without this
support, the text may be too difficult for students to read independently, to fully
comprehend, or to evaluate. The "sharing" of the reading, the modeling by the
teacher, and the focused discussion of the text allow for extensive interaction
between the teacher, the students, and the text.

Using shared reading with older students

One of the major goals of shared reading is to help children develop a range of
effective strategies for reading and understanding text.
Parkes, 2000, page 25

In relation to literacy, it is often stated that students spend the first few years of
school learning to read and the rest of their time reading to learn. This is an
overly simplistic and misleading dichotomy. As soon as small children start
noticing print and recognizing that print holds meaning, they are learning
through reading. We all continue to "learn to read" in that we learn to apply our
reading skills to new and different kinds of texts. The teaching of reading needs
to continue through and beyond the early years of elementary schooling.

Students' reading patterns change as they develop fluency. They become
increasingly knowledgeable about the world through their own direct experiences
as well as through indirect means, such as reading, television, the Internet, and
social contacts. They also learn to see things from different perspectives and
understand that there may be different viewpoints from their own.

At the same time, teachers present increasingly challenging and complex texts
and tasks to their students. They often assume that because their students can
read, they do not have to be taught reading skills. However, the reading
demands on a seven-year-old are very different from those on a twelve-, fifteen-,
or eighteen-year-old student. Problems arise when teachers do not recognize
that their older students may still need instruction in reading complex texts or
understanding on a more sophisticated level.

Coming together for a purpose

Shared reading can be used with all or a part of the class. In either case, it usually requires the students to physically move and sit together. This coming together is for two main purposes. First, everyone must be able to see the text. This ensures that all eyes are on the text at the same time, so the support and interaction can be highly focused. Rather than using individual copies, which can reduce or dilute the focus on the learning, texts for shared reading are usually enlarged in some way. The text used may be an oversized book, chart, or poster, or it may be enlarged by using the overhead projector.

Second, it allows the discussion and the making of meaning to be collaborative. If students are spaced around the room, it is hard to foster a feeling of "working it out together" in a community of learners. Getting together around a book or other text implies – and, in fact, demands – interaction. Literacy learning depends not only on the student's interaction with the text but also on his or her interaction with other people (Vygotsky, 1978; Dowhower, 1999).

When students are physically closer together, they engage in dialogue more readily. They can share and learn more about each other and the worlds they live in and can explore the texts to arrive at deeper understandings. They can make eye contact, use other accepted forms of affirmations or disagreement, and participate in accountable talk far more easily than if they were in separate spaces. It is also easier for the teacher to ask students to have a quick discussion with someone next to them before participating in the larger group. Collaborative or shared learning arrangements promote oral language development and peer support in ways that are often unavailable in more formal learning situations.

See chapter 11 for practical advice on how to manage the arrangements for shared reading.

A theoretical basis for shared reading

Shared reading may have grown from the concept of the bedtime story, but its use as a teaching approach is supported by well-documented research into the learning process. In particular, its use is supported by the closely related notions of the *zone of proximal development, scaffolding*, and the *gradual release of responsibility*. Connecting all three is the recognition that *social interaction* is important for driving the learning process. Shared reading utilizes all these notions to move students toward greater independence as learners.

Zone of proximal development

The concept of the *zone of proximal development* was described by Vygotsky (1978). According to Vygotsky, learning occurs in an area (zone) that is "between the actual developmental level as determined by individual problem solving and the level of potential development as determined through problem solving under adult guidance or in collaboration with more capable peers" (Vygotsky, 1978, page 86). The zone of *actual* development is where an individual can achieve learning independently. The zone of *proximal* development is the area where a more knowledgeable person needs to guide and support the learning. In teaching, this means that the teacher as the expert supports the student in developing their learning. In addition, Vygotsky stressed the need for social interaction to assist learning.

Scaffolding

The support that helps students move through this zone and on to independence has been described as *scaffolding* (Bruner, 1983). The metaphor reflects the temporary nature of the support and its specific purpose. Support (the strength or amount of scaffolding) can be increased or decreased in response to the needs of the students. A commonly used example of this concept is that of a parent teaching a child to ride a bicycle.

Figure 1.1 Decreasing support, increasing independence

Gradual release of responsibility

The closely related notion of the *gradual release of responsibility* (Gallagher and Pearson, 1983) refers to the change that occurs as the teacher carefully withdraws support (dismantles the scaffolding) as the responsibility for learning shifts from the teacher to the student. Teachers subtly adjust the support they give according to the learning they see taking place. As the students master the learning, the teacher withdraws support to the point where the students can regulate or take over the learning for themselves. As new challenges are introduced, teacher support will again be required

In shared reading, the teacher provides strong initial support by reading the text aloud. The teacher extends this support by explaining and showing *how* an expert reader makes meaning from the text. Modeling the use of strategies and thinking aloud about the text are two of the ways in which teachers can provide support. During the lesson, the teacher encourages and helps the students as they try using the strategies themselves and changes the amount of support according to the needs of the group. Throughout the lesson, the teacher and the students are interacting with each other, discussing what they are doing, giving suggestions and feedback, and sharing ideas and opinions. All these interactions help advance the learning and promote the social environment that is necessary for learning.

Learning in a social context

Interaction is an essential part of learning. The social context in which shared reading takes place is critical to its success. In his analysis of talk between children in classrooms, Mercer (1994) shows that interactions happen in different ways. Of the three modes he describes, the mode called *exploratory talk* is the one in which most learning is likely to happen. It involves sharing

information, backing up assertions with reasons, and reaching agreement. Participants show a degree of trust and pool their knowledge to solve problems. Mercer suggests that this mode is the most likely of the three to result in the kind of thinking that moves participants through their zones of proximal development. A good shared reading lesson can encourage this kind of talk.

Holdaway (1979, page 64) states that "corporate experiences of culturally significant language have *always* been powerful modes of learning." By engaging in this interactive, corporate process, students can gain and share the understandings they need to become competent, independent readers. In the context of a shared reading lesson, the student–teacher interactions and the student–student interactions are centered on a text and provide both support and models through which new learning can take place. These interactions also enable students to reflect on *how* they are thinking as well as *what* they are thinking (Braunger and Lewis, 1998).

The teacher acts as a facilitator for the social interactions by leading and encouraging talk that deepens thinking and results in new understandings. Chapter 7 explores some of the ways in which teachers can promote this kind of talk in their shared reading lessons.

Metacognition

Metacognition, which is needed to use comprehension strategies well, can begin during direct teacher explanations and modeling of strategies but develops most completely when students practice using comprehension strategies as they read.

Pressley, 2002, page 292

Within a shared reading approach, teachers provide opportunities for their students to learn about themselves as readers and learners by reflecting on their own thinking. This reflection is part of the concept of *metacognition* which refers to the ways in which we think about our own thinking processes. Metacognition can and should be actively developed.

Keene and Zimmermann (1997) quote Cris Tovani explaining metacognition to her students as "knowing when you know, knowing when you don't, and thinking about your own thinking." She goes on to explain that: "You have to know what you need to know when you are reading and how to solve problems when meaning breaks down. [In other words,] when you get stuck, there are a bunch of things you can do to get unstuck" (pages 195–196).

In shared reading, teachers model ways of "thinking about thinking," including how to get unstuck, to enable their students to do this themselves. Questions, reflections, feedback, and prompts should aim to develop the students' internal dialogue (or self-monitoring).

Shared reading shows students how to use strategies to access and make meaning of any text, not simply to understand the piece of text that has been used that day.

Using shared reading across the curriculum

In many elementary schools, the classroom teacher takes responsibility for most of the curriculum. They may teach math, social studies, and science as well as English language arts. Some elementary schools and most middle schools use specialist teachers for what are called the "content" areas of the curriculum. Specialist teachers tend to assume that their students come to them fully equipped with the skills needed to make sense of the texts and tasks they give them. Unfortunately, this is not the case for large numbers of students. Who is responsible for teaching older students to read? As noted earlier, the demands placed on students as they move up through the school system and engage with different curriculum areas require them to be good readers. Even more, they need to have a high standard of literacy if they are to participate and learn in middle and high school.

Most content area teachers see their primary responsibility as preparing young adolescents and teenagers in their subject area for high school and college, and they have difficulty accepting that they should have some responsibility for adolescents' reading development.

Vacca, 2002, page 186

The reality is that all teachers need to be aware of the reading demands they place on students and be prepared to support their students in meeting such demands. Allington (2002) restates the familiar but often unpopular contention: "In my ideal world every teacher would be a teacher of reading" (page 143). He describes how all teachers, particularly in the middle and high school years, could help their students by teaching them how texts work and familiarizing them with the vocabulary specific to different subjects. They could also help by selecting texts that are "well written and of appropriate levels of complexity given the students' prior knowledge as well as their levels of literacy" (Allington, 2002, page 143).

Many teachers already use forms of reading instruction in their content area teaching. They may go over a section of a textbook with their students, summarize and/or highlight main ideas, or teach new vocabulary. Some teachers use a form of shared reading for these kinds of instruction. Shared reading can be used to simultaneously unlock the meaning in a text and teach the integration and application of strategies that students can apply to the next piece of text.

The framework for explicit instruction described in chapter 9 is useful for content area teaching. The stages of explaining, modeling, guided practice, student demonstration, and independent use can all be included in content area teaching to scaffold students' learning of how to read informational texts as well helping them to understand, synthesize, and evaluate the information itself. Vacca (2002) emphasizes the importance of supporting students before, during, and after content-area reading. He describes ways in which these "invisible" aspects of teaching can be used to improve learning outcomes for students.

Shared reading offers all teachers an approach within which support can be provided. The examples in this book demonstrate ways in which both classroom and specialist teachers have incorporated shared reading into their teaching.

> *The teacher's role is to provide the readers with a range of appropriate strategies by modeling, discussion, and direct instruction.*
>
> Smith and Elley, 1997, page 53

The pedagogy: explicit teaching in shared reading

Margaret Mooney (1988) noted that the teacher's role in shared reading consists of showing students what reading can do for them and how they can be readers, encouraging them to participate in readings, and responding to their efforts. In shared reading, the students are supported at several levels. In a shared reading session, the students are exposed to:

- the modeling of fluent reading;

- an expert reader's demonstration of the "thinking work" that occurs during reading;

- the modeling of strategies such as predicting, questioning the text, making inferences, and the use of word-level strategies;

- the ideas, concepts, topics, themes, and features of a wider variety of texts than they would be able to read for themselves.

When the teacher initiates and fosters interaction about a text, the students have opportunities to:

- share their thoughts and feelings about the text;

- discuss their ideas, questions, and understandings;

- make and revise their own predictions;

- share their own experiences that relate to the text;

- make and share connections with other texts and with what they know of the wider world;

- practice the strategies the teacher has demonstrated or modeled;

- debate opinions within a safe environment;

- make meaning through the text, the discussion, and their reflections with the teacher and their peers;

- develop awareness of their own thinking;

- internalize their thought processes so that they become automatic.

Although these teaching and learning functions can be carried out in many different ways, shared reading provides teachers with more options in their teaching. The support provided through shared learning helps the students to learn ways of handling texts that they can use later with less support, such as in guided reading or further shared reading lessons. The nature of the support can be adjusted to meet the varying needs of the students – even within one session.

Revisiting familiar texts, talking about reading, and thinking about depth of meaning are central to learning about the reading process (Koskinen, Blum, Bisson, Phillips, Creamer, and Baker, 1999; Oster, 2001; Pressley, 1998; Williams, 2001). Shared reading provides opportunities for all these processes.

Shared reading and the diversity of learners

We must make sure that students of diverse backgrounds have the opportunity to participate in literature-based instruction and the readers' workshop, following a continuum of teaching strategies that involves them in motivating, meaningful reading experiences.

Au, 2002, page 409

Students come from many different backgrounds. Teachers need to take into account the diverse aspects of the students' home cultures, for example:

- the language traditions (oral, written, visual);

- the kinds of knowledge valued (the teacher should learn about and be able to build on the knowledge that all students bring to the school setting, especially when that knowledge is very different from the teacher's);

- the child–adult behaviors that are valued (for example, in some cultures, it is not appropriate for young people to offer an opinion to an adult or to comment critically on a text);

- the expectations around speaking or displaying knowledge to a group (for example, for some students, the "trying out" encouraged in shared reading does not sit comfortably with the need to "get it right");

- whether the diversity represented in the classroom and the wider community is reflected in the texts used in the classroom (texts need to affirm the identities of the students).

The starting point should always be what the students already know and can do. Consequently, the texts and purposes selected for shared reading should reflect the student diversity as well as meeting curriculum requirements and other external expectations.

English language learners

The high degree of interaction and sharing of ideas between students that should take place in shared reading means that English language learners will be exposed to English in a supportive context.

Students learning English need a great deal of exposure to supported reading to develop the background knowledge they need (including knowledge of how the language works) to make accurate predictions as they read. Shared reading enables support to be given in natural, non-stigmatizing ways.

In the older grades, shared reading may be used as a form of small-group instruction that may be more effective in meeting English language learners' needs than, for example, guided reading. Shared reading allows students to actively participate in rereadings, to hear and participate in fluent reading, and to learn from more explicit modeling by the teacher and peers. The approach enables the teacher to direct questions or comments to specific students and to modify the challenge or support according to their needs. For example, the teacher may increase the level of support by rereading key points or words. Teachers need to change their approach if their students encounter difficulties when reading in English. When asking the students to predict what is to be read, they will need to provide support using illustrations or photographs, layout clues, the title, and other meanings and structures.

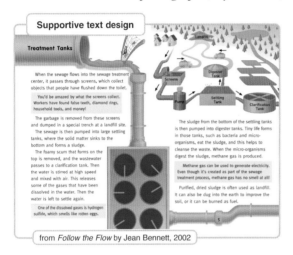

from *Follow the Flow* by Jean Bennett, 2002

Because shared reading is such a valuable approach when working with students who are learning English, the teacher should take extra care to choose texts that are relevant and appropriate to the age group. "Labeled" books, such as picture dictionaries or books designed for younger readers, are not always useful because they have limited vocabulary and do not always model a wide variety of sentence structures. Books are available that include age appropriate photographs and diagrams along with straightforward text designed to support language learning.

Texts about experiences familiar to the students will provide opportunities to develop language, share experiences, and build up a field of knowledge. These could include recipes, menus, advertisements, or cards and announcements about celebrations and community events, family life, sport, and fashion. The materials must have strong graphic support and clear text.

Shared writing also gives strong support to new users of English while validating and building on their own knowledge and experiences. See chapter 10 for a discussion of the connections between shared reading and writing.

Struggling readers

Research has shown the effectiveness of shared reading at grade 2 level as an intervention to improve reading proficiency. "After four months, students in the shared book experience classrooms had better word analysis performance, better comprehension of materials read, and the fluency of both groups improved." (Allington, 2001, page 81). Such strong demonstration of the value of shared reading with struggling readers could be taken as reason enough for using the approach at all grade levels. As well as improving proficiency, shared reading can boost motivation and improve self-esteem with students who struggle to decode or make sense of the materials they are expected to read in grade 3 and beyond. Careful text selection, differentiated questioning (see chapter 7), and the support provided by teacher and peers make it possible for the struggling readers to access far more meaning and strategies than they would be able to manage on their own. Repeated readings and the modeling of good reading by an expert also promote fluency. Lack of fluency in their reading is one of the major factors that can turn slow readers into struggling readers (Pressley, 2002; Allington, 2001).

Shared reading makes difficult texts and concepts accessible to all students in a group or class, and all students – including those from diverse backgrounds – can participate confidently because they are able to construct their own meaning with the support of the teacher and the other readers.

CHAPTER 2

Shared Reading in the Literacy Program

Approaches to literacy instruction

An effective literacy program provides opportunities every day for students to talk, listen, read, and write. Teachers also expect students to view and discuss a wide variety of texts. An effective teacher adjusts and balances activities according to the needs of individual students and uses them for explicitly stated purposes. Learning is most effective if it builds on and links with what the students can already do.

Reading approaches or practices in an effective literacy program may include:

- reading aloud to students (Fountas and Pinnell, 2001);

- shared reading (Holdaway, 1980; Parkes, 2000; Routman, 2000);

- guided or small-group reading instruction (Learning Media Limited, 2000; Fountas and Pinnell, 2001);

- reciprocal teaching (Palincsar and Brown, 1985);

- literature circles (Daniels, 1994);

- cooperative learning (Johnson, Johnson, and Holubec, 1993);

- transactional strategies instruction (Pressley 2002);

- shared read aloud (Routman, 2002);

- independent reading (Clay, 1991);

- reading workshops (Calkins, 2001);

- mini-lessons (Calkins, 2001).

A balanced literacy program

"Balanced literacy" has come to mean a classroom program that includes a variety of approaches and activities. These range from modeling, where the teacher does the reading and writing for the students, to independent activities, where the students do almost all the reading and writing themselves. A balanced literacy program at any grade level will provide many opportunities for reading and writing to, with, and by the students. Shared reading and guided reading are closely related approaches where the teacher reads with the students as they work out texts together. If these aspects of a literacy program are overlooked, students miss out on the valuable support that bridges their learning from the teacher to their own internal control. It is a concern for renewed emphasis on reading *with* students, through the use of shared reading, that has driven this book.

Writing is, of course, an integral part of the classroom literacy program and can be taught using similar approaches to reading. The ways in which the reciprocal nature of reading and writing can be enhanced by shared reading are discussed in chapter 10.

The choices that teachers make about which approaches they use in the literacy program often reflect two complementary and dynamic imperatives. One is the need to gradually release responsibility for learning from the teacher to the student. The other is the need to increase the challenges to enable the student to make progress and keep learning alive. Both of these teaching and learning imperatives continue throughout schooling: there is no end point at which any learner knows it all, or beyond which there are no new challenges.

Shared reading is an approach that allows teachers to give support when students face a new or significant challenge in their learning. For example, fluent readers who are presented with a challenging new topic in science may require support until they are able to use the text independently. Through shared reading, the teacher may model and explain how to read the text by teaching the specialist vocabulary, by showing the students how they can make connections with what they already know, and by giving them opportunities to practice using these strategies. As the students become confident, they are able to take more responsibility for their own learning. Eventually, with subtle changes to the nature of the support (which could include small-group and independent practice time), the students will also be able to integrate their new knowledge of the topic and of effective reading strategies.

Learning does not stop here though. Teachers should always be presenting their students with challenges, such as new topics, more complex vocabulary or text structures, and more sophisticated content.

Shared reading across age levels

Students differ greatly in their reading development, and the comparisons below are indicative, not prescriptive.[1] As successful adult readers, teachers need to remember that reading is a learned and taught skill. The teaching of reading needs to be planned, deliberate, and built on the growing and changing needs of students.

[1] These comparisons are based on the concept of a developmental continuum, such as that in *First Steps* (Education Department of Western Australia, 1997).

Figure 2.1 Age level comparisons

Age: 5 to 7	Age: 8 to 10	Age: 11 to 13
Purposes • To foster the enjoyment of reading a wide variety of texts • To teach how books and print work • To encourage the discovery and sharing of meaning • To teach about sounds, letters, and words • To model the use and practice of cues to make meaning • To provide support in the co-construction of meaning • To develop and extend reading repertoire • To develop oral language and vocabulary • To provide models for writing • To foster community building	**Purposes** • To extend enjoyment of reading for a variety of purposes • To extend knowledge of how books and text types work • To provide support in the co-construction of meaning • To model the use, integration, and practice of reading strategies • To model strategies for deepening comprehension • To develop and extend vocabulary • To provide models for writing • To provide opportunities for studying writers' craft • To provide opportunities for accessing meaning in different content areas	**Purposes** • To motivate students to value and enjoy reading a wide variety of texts • To deepen understanding of text formats and structures • To provide support in the co-construction of meaning • To help students explore a wide variety of texts across content areas • To model strategies for unraveling dense, complex, or ambiguous texts • To allow for identifying and exploring multiple genres within a piece of text • To provide opportunities for evaluating texts • To allow students to synthesize information • To develop students' skills and habits of thinking and responding critically • To encourage students to challenge the authority of texts • To help students to determine and compare authors' purposes, points of view, and biases • To have students analyze writing styles and effects • To provide models for writing • To deepen students' understanding of the power of literacy and literature
Suggested text formats and types • Big books of stories, plays, poems, nonfiction • Posters, charts • Poem cards • Class-made big books, posters, and charts • Rhythmic, rhyming, and repetitive texts • Electronic and visual texts	**Suggested text formats and types** • Big books • Posters, charts • Poems, songs, diagrams • Short enlarged extracts from longer texts, such as novels, articles, short stories, text books • Newspaper and magazine articles • Electronic and visual texts • Students' writing • Texts on overhead transparencies	**Suggested text formats and types** • Short enlarged extracts from novels, textbooks, and other sources • Newspaper and magazine articles • Short stories, journals, letters • Poems, plays • Public or historical documents (facsimiles) • Maps, charts, diagrams, tables • Brochures, advertisements • Posters, cartoons • Students' writing • Texts on overhead transparencies

Age: 5 to 7	Age: 8 to 10	Age: 11 to 13
Physical arrangements	**Physical arrangements**	**Physical arrangements**
• Students seated on a rug or carpeted floor close to the teacher so that all can see the text	• Students seated in a group on carpeted floor, or on seats in a meeting area so that all can see the text	• Students at own desks or tables or in designated meeting area
• Book placed on an easel	• Text placed on easel, attached to wall, or projected from an overhead projector	• Teacher using overhead projector, charts, and posters
• Long pointer used to point to text as it is read		• Essential that all can see the text
• Whiteboard or chart paper nearby for teaching points	• Whiteboard, chart paper, graphic organizers available if needed for teaching points	• Whiteboard, chart paper, graphic organizers available if needed for teaching points
• Magnetic letters available for letter and word study	• Pointer used to help students to follow text or used to point out specific parts of the text	• Highlighter pen or tape to aid focus on vocabulary, terms, text features, or concepts
• "Window" cards and removable tape to cover or expose words or letters for close study	• Highlighter pen or tape to aid focus on words, phrases, or sections of the text	

Shared reading and reading aloud

Reading aloud to students has sound educational benefits and is generally popular with students. It's important at all ages because it enables students to enjoy books they might not be able to access on their own, thus deepening and increasing the extent of their reading repertoire. It also allows for joint and meaningful ongoing discussion in the classroom and develops a body of knowledge and experience within a class. As discussed in a later chapter, knowledge about a new topic can be built through reading relevant books aloud to the class.

The purpose of the teacher reading aloud is often simply to involve students in "a good read" and to let them enjoy a wide variety of texts read by an expert reader. Teachers model fluent and expressive reading. Reading aloud to students immerses them in and exposes them to different patterns of language, such as those in fables, mysteries, classic literature, poetry, and the many varieties of nonfiction.

Reading aloud and shared reading have obvious overlaps, and some teachers skillfully move between the two approaches to highlight a feature or focus on a specific teaching point while reading a book aloud. Such teaching points are, of course, linked to the needs of the students. In the example that follows, the teacher used a short excerpt from a novel he was reading aloud to the class. He

copied it onto an overhead transparency for shared reading. Using part of a text
that the students had already listened to enabled the teacher to focus on the
author's techniques. It also allowed the students to place this excerpt in a context.

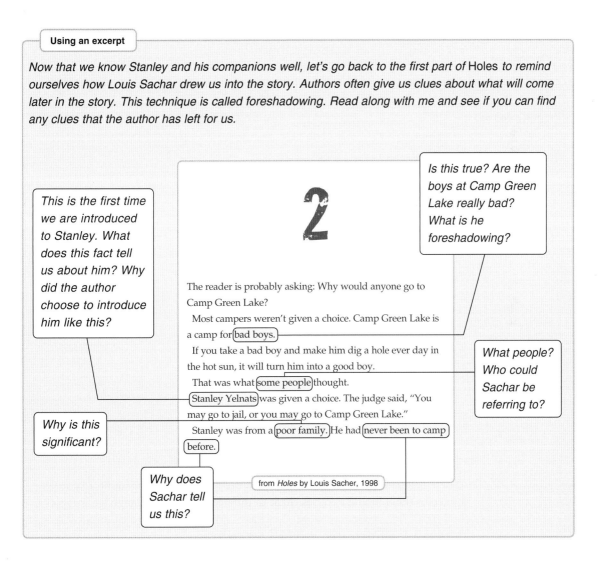

Using an excerpt

Now that we know Stanley and his companions well, let's go back to the first part of Holes *to remind ourselves how Louis Sachar drew us into the story. Authors often give us clues about what will come later in the story. This technique is called foreshadowing. Read along with me and see if you can find any clues that the author has left for us.*

Is this true? Are the boys at Camp Green Lake really bad? What is he foreshadowing?

This is the first time we are introduced to Stanley. What does this fact tell us about him? Why did the author choose to introduce him like this?

The reader is probably asking: Why would anyone go to Camp Green Lake?

Most campers weren't given a choice. Camp Green Lake is a camp for bad boys.

If you take a bad boy and make him dig a hole ever day in the hot sun, it will turn him into a good boy.

That was what some people thought.

Stanley Yelnats was given a choice. The judge said, "You may go to jail, or you may go to Camp Green Lake."

Stanley was from a poor family. He had never been to camp before.

What people? Who could Sachar be referring to?

Why is this significant?

Why does Sachar tell us this?

from *Holes* by Louis Sacher, 1998

23

As students move up through the school, teachers change the nature of the challenges in discussion as they read aloud, questioning the author's purpose and style, uncovering themes and features of different texts, and modeling such strategies as making predictions, checking for meaning, and making inferences. Variations on this practice may be called "think aloud" (Baumann, Jones, and Seifert-Kessell, 1993), "shared reading aloud" (Routman, 2002), or "interactive read aloud" (Fountas and Pinnell, 2001).

Figure 2.2 Shared reading and reading aloud

Shared reading	Reading aloud
• All eyes are on the same text.	• The teacher reads from a single copy of the text, which the students usually cannot see.
• The teacher is the expert reader. The students follow with their eyes on the text. They may also read aloud.	• The teacher is the expert reader while the students listen.
• Texts may be more difficult than all or some could read or use independently.	• Texts may be more difficult than all or some could read or use independently.
• The teacher provides a strong level of support for making meaning.	• The amount of discussion depends on the teacher's purpose and the students' needs: it varies from a little to a lot.
• The approach features student discussion, problem solving, interaction, negotiation, and navigation of meaning.	• The texts are selected primarily for the students' enjoyment and to increase their exposure to a variety of literature or nonfiction.
• The approach has specific teaching purposes that involve modeling and integrating strategies to make meaning.	• The approach exposes the students to a variety of concepts, themes, ideas, new vocabulary, and language structures.
• The text is selected to match the purpose.	• The texts may be fiction (novels, stories, picture books) or nonfiction (biography, memoirs, descriptions, scientific texts).
• The approach involves a very wide variety of text types in fiction and nonfiction.	
• The approach exposes the students to a variety of concepts, themes, ideas, new words, and text structures.	
• The nature of support varies depending on the needs of the students.	

Shared reading and guided reading

These two approaches have much in common: both focus on constructing meaning and developing students' comprehension. However, there is a clear distinction between them. In shared reading, the teacher takes initial responsibility for the reading: he or she reads the text aloud. The students can all see the text, which is usually enlarged. The teacher is "thinking aloud" and modeling the strategies that lead to reading fluently with comprehension.

In guided reading, the teacher supports the students as they read the text themselves. The teacher's role is to establish the purpose, introduce the text to the group, and observe and support the students as they read silently. Integral parts of the session are the discussion of the text to ensure comprehension, the practice of strategies, and the encouragement of responses from the students. The teacher decides whether to use shared or guided reading for a particular group of students by examining the challenges of the selected text. If the students will need substantial support to read the text, shared reading is more appropriate than guided reading. At times, even easily readable texts can and should be used for shared reading so that they can be enjoyed by the classroom community.

Shared reading does not always have to be done as a whole-class lesson. For example, with students who are learning English, shared reading in a small-group situation can be more effective than guided reading because it allows fluent reading to be modeled and developed. Shared reading also provides access to a wide variety of texts, which is important for building knowledge and vocabulary with English language learners.

Figure 2.3 Shared reading and guided reading

Shared reading	Guided reading
• The teacher works with a whole class or a group.	• The teacher works with a small group (four to eight students).
• Enlarged text is used (all eyes on same text).	• The teacher sets a purpose for the lesson.
• The reading difficulty is not critical – it may be greater than most or some could read independently.	• Every participant has a copy of the same text.
• The text may be familiar.	• The text is carefully selected to be at the group's instructional level.
• The teacher reads the text aloud. The students follow silently or verbally.	• The students have usually not seen the text before.
• The text selected is specific to the students' learning needs.	• The teacher introduces the text and supports the students' thinking and reading.
• The teacher sets a purpose for the lesson.	• The students read the text individually, usually silently.
• The teacher models new learning.	• The text provides a carefully selected balance of supports and challenges specific to the students' learning needs.
• The teacher leads the class or group construction of meaning,	• The approach allows the practice of skills and strategies already introduced.
• The teacher models fluent reading and strategy use.	• The group takes over the construction of meaning from the teacher.
• The text provides a carefully selected balance of supports and challenges specific to the students' learning needs.	

Shared reading and mini-lessons

Mini-lessons grew out of Donald Graves' workshop approach to teaching writing (Graves, 1983) and are described in Calkins (2001). Although in many ways they may be similar to shared reading, there are some important differences. A key difference is the focus. In shared reading, the focus is on reading a specific text for a specific purpose. In a mini-lesson, the focus is usually a specific teaching point. Immediately after the mini-lesson, the students are usually given opportunities to practice the teaching point that has been presented. Calkins (2001) calls this opportunity to "have a go" the "active involvement phase" (page 84). For example, at the beginning of the school year, many teachers do several mini-lessons on one or all of the following:

- How can we choose "just right books"?

- How can we sustain our reading for longer periods of time?

- What are some ways that our reading buddies can help each other?

Students are expected to work on applying what they learn in the mini-lessons and then follow up their learning by sharing their experiences.

The similarities between shared reading and mini-lessons include teacher demonstration and modeling and the importance of the discussion between the teacher and the students. The ultimate purpose of both shared reading and mini-lessons is to prepare students for taking more control of their own reading and use of texts.

Figure 2.4 Shared reading and reading mini-lesson

Shared reading	Reading mini-lesson
• The approach is text centered with all eyes on the same text. • A session lasts about fifteen to thirty minutes. • The reading experience may be self-contained. • The main focus is reading or working through a specific text for a purpose.	• The lesson is not necessarily text centered: the teacher may read a short text or extract aloud, use an enlarged text, or not use a text at all. • A lesson lasts about five to fifteen minutes. • It is always linked to previous and following reading experiences and activities. • The main focus is that of teaching a specific reading or comprehension strategy or task.

Other practices

Why not round robin reading?

Round robin reading is where all the students have access to the same text and take turns at reading sections of it aloud. The teacher calls on individual students to each read a specified paragraph, page, or chapter. The reading then passes to the next student selected or the next student in the row or circle. The text is usually one that the students have not seen before.

Is this shared reading? Many teachers believe that it is. Technically, the task of reading is indeed shared among the participants, but the meaning is often lost for a variety of reasons. There are serious disadvantages to this practice that make it unacceptable in any reading program. When students are called on to read an unfamiliar text out loud to a group of peers, their attention almost always becomes focused on getting the words right rather than on understanding what they are reading (Worthy and Broaddus, 2002). Further, reading an unfamiliar text to an audience may not encourage risk-taking or self-monitoring – both essential skills for all readers to learn (Opitz and Rasinski, 1998). For those waiting their turn, the focus is usually on reading ahead to find out when their turn will come. Some anxious students may even be practicing their part as they wait for their turn or be planning to take a bathroom break. For those who have already had their turn, there is a strong tendency to either switch off ("Whew – that's done!") or, if they are interested in the text, to read on ahead of the oral reading.

This highlights another problem with round robin reading – that of the different rates at which people read. Trying to follow along with a slow or halting reader not only impedes comprehension but may also encourage poor, disjointed reading habits in the listeners (Opitz and Rasinski, 1998).

The message is clear: this is not shared reading, it is not guided reading, and it is not good practice in any reading program.

Choral reading

Reading in chorus is not shared reading either. At times, choral reading may be appropriate when students read a poem or similar text aloud together. This kind of reading is primarily for performance and is not considered to be an instructional reading practice. Skillfully directed, it can improve the fluency and expression of students' reading. During shared reading, students may read a piece of text together out loud, but this is usually not the main focus of the lesson.

CHAPTER 3

Texts for Shared Reading

Learning never stops

This chapter focuses on selecting and using texts for shared reading, including shared reading in content areas. In this book the word "text" is used as a generic term to include any written, printed, or electronically transmitted material that uses words and/or images to convey meaning.

In the process of finding and creating meaning in texts, students need ongoing opportunities to develop and modify their expectations of and about reading and writing.

The texts selected for shared reading must reflect this ongoing process. They must represent the widest possible variety of genres, topics, text types, themes, and purposes, which reflect the curriculum and the demands that students will face in their academic and personal reading.

Challenges and supports

In planning a shared reading lesson, teachers make decisions that reflect three interrelated aspects of each lesson:

- the students (their interests, knowledge, and needs);

- the purpose or objective (what the teacher wants the students to learn);

- the text (its suitability in regard to both the students and the objectives).

To do this, teachers must be able to assess the supports and challenges that the text will provide for their students.

Supports are the features that readers use to help them make meaning: they make the text easy for that reader. Challenges are the features that make a text difficult for a particular reader. It is impossible to identify challenges and supports in isolation because, by definition, they depend on the knowledge and experiences of the reader.

Figure 3.1 Aspects of text selection

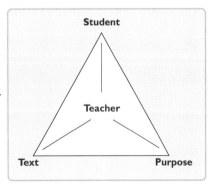

Features that are challenges for some students may be supports for others. For example, the use of a cut-away diagram will support students who can visualize a whole object from seeing a section. But it may confuse students who have less experience with diagrams and who find it difficult to visualize a whole from a part. Teachers who know their students well can adjust their support for different students. Adjusting that support can be done easily in a shared reading lesson and ensures that all students can access the text.

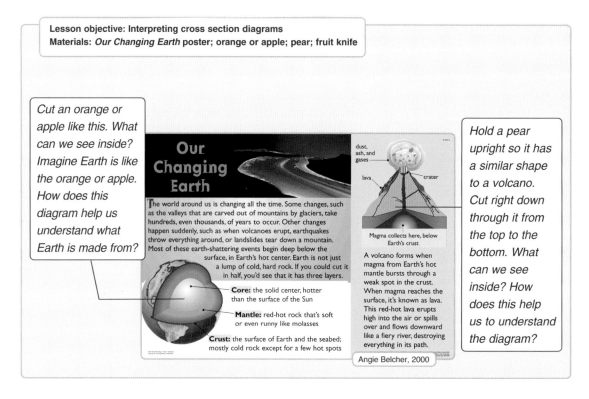

Lesson objective: Interpreting cross section diagrams
Materials: *Our Changing Earth* poster; orange or apple; pear; fruit knife

Cut an orange or apple like this. What can we see inside? Imagine Earth is like the orange or apple. How does this diagram help us understand what Earth is made from?

Our Changing Earth

The world around us is changing all the time. Some changes, such as the valleys that are carved out of mountains by glaciers, take hundreds, even thousands, of years to occur. Other changes happen suddenly, such as when volcanoes erupt, earthquakes throw everything around, or landslides tear down a mountain. Most of these earth-shattering events begin deep below the surface, in Earth's hot center. Earth is not just a lump of cold, hard rock. If you could cut it in half, you'd see that it has three layers.

Core: the solid center, hotter than the surface of the Sun

Mantle: red-hot rock that's soft or even runny like molasses

Crust: the surface of Earth and the seabed; mostly cold rock except for a few hot spots

dust, ash, and gases

lava

crater

Magma collects here, below Earth's crust

A volcano forms when magma from Earth's hot mantle bursts through a weak spot in the crust. When magma reaches the surface, it's known as lava. This red-hot lava erupts high into the air or spills over and flows downward like a fiery river, destroying everything in its path.

Angie Belcher, 2000

Hold a pear upright so it has a similar shape to a volcano. Cut right down through it from the top to the bottom. What can we see inside? How does this help us to understand the diagram?

The challenges in a text are not limited to the surface features, such as individual words, images, or the layout. In fact, in the upper grades, it is often the deeper levels of meaning that provide the challenges. Valerie, a grade 6 teacher, selected the following poem to use with her class. She chose it because although it's an easy text to decode and the topic is familiar, her students often have trouble in identifying the mood created by an author.

Valerie shows the poem on an overhead transparency and covers the text so that only the title can be seen.

The purpose of today's lesson is to explore how an author creates a mood. When I approach a poem for the first time, I look at the title and think about how it might relate to me. I had to move a lot as a kid, and although there was always a little bit of excitement, I mostly remember feeling scared and sad.

- *What does "new house" mean to you?*

The discussion reveals that the students have different experiences with moving and different associations with "new houses." Valerie then prompts their thinking with the following:

- *Why do we have different responses to the title?*

- *Think about a time you've seen an empty house. What feelings does an empty house evoke for you? What images come to mind?*

New House

The first time I saw you
You lay empty
Desolate, bare, abandoned
Your long halls scared me
Your wide open spaces kept me silent
You smelt musty, dust went right through me
Colors shivered upon your walls
Waiting to see life
Your windows and doors
Cupboards and carpets
All watched me, waiting for signs of approval
Now your rooms are my rooms
And we share my free time
I hang my clothes in your closet
And you hold and protect me as I sleep

Amy Wilson, 2000

Now I'm going to read the poem twice. Once so you can pick up the mood or overall feeling of the poem, and a second time so I can show you what the author did to create that mood. Please follow along with me …

During the second reading, Valerie pauses to focus on the author's choice of words.

- *The author chose to use the word "desolate." Why? What does it mean?*

- *What else is desolate? What does it make you think of?*

Valerie highlights other significant words as she reads, showing how they connect with her prior knowledge and how they help her to create images. The class then explores together the mood of the poem and how the author crafted it, using the following discussion points:

- *How has your interpretation of the title changed now that you've read the poem?*

- *How was your reading of the poem influenced by your own experiences?*

- *What words and images have been most important in creating the mood?*

- *How did the author's feelings change during the course of the poem? How does the mood of the poem change as a result?*

Valerie highlights key words on the overhead transparency and then asks the students to discuss the impact of the chosen words and images.

Texts can be used for different purposes, which may require a more sophisticated understanding of the text. The challenges can come not so much from the text itself but from the ways in which the students have to use the text. The example below shows a historical account that was a relatively easy read for a group. However, when they were asked to use it to make a timeline, some students found it hard to isolate the important information. A shared reading approach was used to show the students how to read the text in order to identify the milestones.

Isolating important information

After reading the text aloud, Simon asked his students to identify the significant events. He prompted them with questions like "What happened first? What happened next?" He then used the following prompts to guide the class in creating a timeline:

- *Skim through the text to get a sense of how many events we will need on our timeline. What's your estimate?*
- *A clue in the first paragraph tells us where to begin our timeline. What words helped you find this?*

GETTING IT THERE

The first postal service was started by the ancient Egyptians around four thousand years ago. The mail was carried by a **network** of messengers.

In early Europe and America, messengers carried mail on foot or on horseback. In the 1700s, people began to send mail from England to America by sea. The invention of the steamship and the train made sending mail even faster.

In 1840, the world's first stick-on stamps were sold in Britain. These stamps were called penny blacks. For a penny, a letter could be delivered anywhere in the country.

Mail was first sent by air in 1911. The first airmail service began in 1919 between England and France. Today, a letter can travel to the other side of the world by air in less than twenty-four hours.

from *Looking at Letters* by John Lockyer, 2000

- *How shall we design our timeline so that we can fit in all the important events and times?*
- *How far apart should the years be?*
- *What year should we start with?*
- *How should we end our timeline?*

To help his students generalize these skills, Simon followed up the lesson with these questions:

- *What have we learned about identifying sequence in a historical account?*
- *What clues does the author give us about the order of events?*
- *What can you tell me about creating your own timeline?*
- *How will these skills help you as a reader?*

If, for a particular group of students, the challenges in a selected text outweigh the supports (even with the added support of the teacher), the piece is too difficult. This can be observed when the shared reading session goes for too long with the teacher valiantly trying to explain the meaning of every word and concept. Likewise, if the supports outweigh the challenges, the piece is too easy, and the students' learning will not be enhanced.

Factors that affect the supports and challenges of any text include:

- the language of the text;

- the experiences and knowledge of the students;

- the cultures of the students;

- the concepts in the text;

- the amount of abstraction and complexity of ideas;

- the text layout and visual features;

- the strategies required to read the text;

- the students' familiarity with a particular genre or form;

- the purposes for which the students are expected to use the text.

The challenge of complex texts

When faced with long, complex texts (such as a social studies or science textbook), many teachers will photocopy a section and give each student a copy to look at as they work through it together. This method can be time-consuming and wasteful. Furthermore, many students get lost and tune out before the lesson is over. This is not shared reading. It is far better to use a small piece of text that has many of the features that students need to learn to manage. Then, in a whole-class shared reading lesson everyone can be taught some strategies that they can apply when they come to the textbook. A series of shared reading lessons can be planned specifically to teach techniques for working with long, complex texts.

Some of the strategies include:

- Using headings, subheadings, and keywords to identify the main ideas in a small piece of text.

- Using a graphic organizer to make notes about what is important, section by section.

- Using picture–text matches to gain more information than a picture or the words would have yielded on their own. (See the example on page 49.)

- Learning how to navigate complex sentences. (For example, the teacher can model writing out and physically cutting up long sentences based on the punctuation and the words that indicate clauses and subclauses.)

- Using questions to clarify what the readers should know when they have read a section. (For example, "The subheading says 'Hunters and Gatherers.' Who hunted and gathered? What did they hunt and gather?")

- Employing a jigsaw approach where small groups work out a short piece of text using the strategies described above. Each group's summary can be written onto a large chart so that an entire chapter is reduced to a series of brief summaries. A shared reading approach is then used to convey each group's learning to the class.

Reading nonfiction

Research shows that until very recently, informational texts have played little or no part in early years of literacy instruction … Not surprisingly, when students are introduced to science and social studies textbooks for the first time in third grade, many of them experience some difficulties reading and comprehending these new kinds of texts.

Parkes, B. in Hoyt, Mooney, and Parkes, 2003, page 19

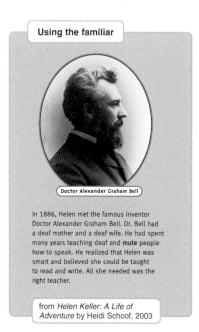

Using the familiar

(Doctor Alexander Graham Bell)

In 1886, Helen met the famous inventor Doctor Alexander Graham Bell. Dr. Bell had a deaf mother and a deaf wife. He had spent many years teaching deaf and **mute** people how to speak. He realized that Helen was smart and believed she could be taught to read and write. All she needed was the right teacher.

from *Helen Keller: A Life of Adventure* by Heidi Schoof, 2003

For many readers, nonfiction provides a sense of excitement and discovery that motivates them to keep reading. For others, however, unfamiliar formats and topics may present barriers to reading.

Fiction and nonfiction texts often need to be read in different ways even though readers use many of the same strategies. A series of shared reading lessons can focus on comparing and contrasting the features of different forms. Teachers can lead their students to use what they know about fiction to help them explore a nonfiction text. For example, if the teacher points out that a biography reads like a fictional story, the students will be able to use their knowledge of story sequence to predict the chronological flow of the text.

Unpacking an informational text

Familiar text features, such as the charts in these examples, support students as they tackle increasingly complex nonfiction texts.

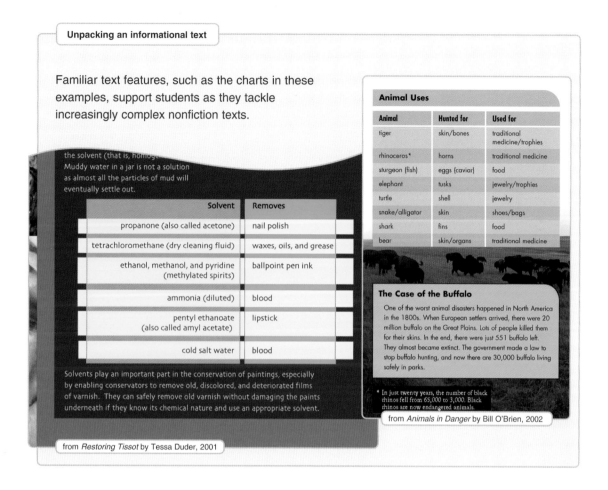

the solvent (that is, homog... Muddy water in a jar is not a solution as almost all the particles of mud will eventually settle out.

Solvent	Removes
propanone (also called acetone)	nail polish
tetrachloromethane (dry cleaning fluid)	waxes, oils, and grease
ethanol, methanol, and pyridine (methylated spirits)	ballpoint pen ink
ammonia (diluted)	blood
pentyl ethanoate (also called amyl acetate)	lipstick
cold salt water	blood

Solvents play an important part in the conservation of paintings, especially by enabling conservators to remove old, discolored, and deteriorated films of varnish. They can safely remove old varnish without damaging the paints underneath if they know its chemical nature and use an appropriate solvent.

from *Restoring Tissot* by Tessa Duder, 2001

Animal Uses

Animal	Hunted for	Used for
tiger	skin/bones	traditional medicine/trophies
rhinoceros*	horns	traditional medicine
sturgeon (fish)	eggs (caviar)	food
elephant	tusks	jewelry/trophies
turtle	shell	jewelry
snake/alligator	skin	shoes/bags
shark	fins	food
bear	skin/organs	traditional medicine

The Case of the Buffalo

One of the worst animal disasters happened in North America in the 1800s. When European settlers arrived, there were 20 million buffalo on the Great Plains. Lots of people killed them for their skins. In the end, there were just 551 buffalo left. They almost became extinct. The government made a law to stop buffalo hunting, and now there are 30,000 buffalo living safely in parks.

* In just twenty years, the number of black rhinos fell from 65,000 to 3,000. Black rhinos are now endangered animals.

from *Animals in Danger* by Bill O'Brien, 2002

Similarly, students can discover how to use familiar text features (table of contents, headings, illustrations) to unpack the denser material of an informational text. Because the specialized vocabulary and organizational features of nonfiction may make the writing less accessible than fiction, students who find nonfiction difficult will have to be shown how to use the familiar to help them tackle the challenges of nonfiction materials.

In addition, technology has enabled designers to present information in graphic forms that may be new to many teachers. The explosion of information available through the Internet, with no constraints or checks on truth, bias, or reliability, offers still more challenges to students and teachers. The task of the teacher has become more complex on two levels: teachers must not only help their students analyze complex texts and text forms but also help them to develop the skills to critique and evaluate information from an enormous variety of sources. The reader's task is to understand what is written or shown graphically in a nonfiction text, to sift and sort for reliable information, and to use this information for various purposes.

Teaching about text features

Features such as a contents page, index, and glossary are familiar to most students by the time they reach third grade. Features of nonfiction texts that may not be so familiar include fact boxes, pullouts, captions, the use of multigenres, alphabetically ordered information, speech or thought bubbles, footnotes, and references. Shared reading can be used to teach students increasingly sophisticated ways of using the features of complex texts. The ways in which texts are structured can be taught to help students understand informational texts and to give them tools to use when searching for specific information. Teachers using an enlarged copy of a page from a text can use shared reading to model how to read the text and use its features for specific purposes (based on identified student needs). These purposes include:

- predicting content;
- searching for specific topics;
- searching for specific information or detail;
- discovering what information may not be found in a particular book or article as well as what can be found;
- extending vocabulary and topic knowledge;
- exploring the ways in which text features can indicate the purpose of the text;
- comparing and contrasting texts;
- identifying a sequence of events;
- establishing cause and effect relationships;
- identifying sources of information;
- understanding when to read and use various text features;
- navigating through the text;
- making the meaning of the text clearer.

Using graphic organizers to analyze texts

As well as selecting good fiction and nonfiction texts for shared reading, teachers can find, and share with their students, tools to help them analyze texts. Graphic organizers are a useful way of supporting students as they analyze a text within a shared reading lesson. There are many published examples, and teachers often make their own to suit the purpose of the lesson. They can be used for many different purposes, for example:

- to capture the ideas generated from a shared reading discussion;

- to make the teacher's thinking more visual and explicit to students;

- to track how ideas change over the course of a discussion;

- to analyze the texts being read;

- to chart specific features of texts;

- to organize ideas into categories;

- to provide a model to prompt students' thinking in independent practice;

- to plan for writing.

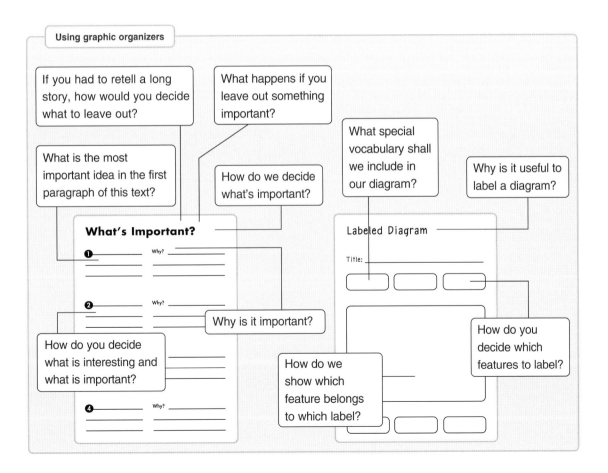

Teaching for visual literacy

Visual literacy is the ability to make meaning from visual texts – texts that may be constructed entirely of images or that may contain images as well as words. Visual texts may include images or information intended to evoke emotions, thoughts, and desires. Pictures and words together are powerful tools, which are used for advertising, cartoons, brochures, websites, charts, and signs.

Visual texts can be found in all parts of our environment. Teaching students visual literacy encourages them to be critical readers of visual texts such as films, magazines, advertising, newspapers, and textbooks.

Exploring visual literacy

In a shared reading lesson on visual literacy, a teacher guided her students to explore this illustration in the following way:

from *There's No Place Like Home* by Mary Leunig, 1992

Today we're going to look at how artists use images to generate emotions, thoughts, feelings, or questions in the viewer. Look closely at this illustration. The first thing I notice is that the creature is standing in a particular pose. He is clearly waiting for someone to show up, and by the way he's looking at his watch, I would guess that he's feeling impatient. My eye is then drawn to the items on the wall. Based on my background knowledge and the connections I'm making between the different parts of the illustration, I now understand that the artist is making a joke. The creature is a case moth who has just emerged from his cocoon. He looks like a guy waiting for his date to show up.

Artists often rely on unexpected connections between images and double meanings to create humor or subtly suggest irony. The viewer often has to do some interpretation work to get the joke. Now that I've shared my schema and associations, can you get the artist's joke?

- *What are some other cartoons, illustrations, and advertisements that use contrasting images or "inside jokes" to create humor?*
- *How do you use your prior knowledge of a comic or cartoon to help you interpret a new one in the series?*
- *Can you give me an example of advertisements that use references to popular culture to target a specific audience?*
- *Why might your grandparents have trouble understanding an ad for skateboards?*

Reading visual texts critically

A New York department store ad, appearing in a September newspaper, shows an image of a ram's horn. The accompanying text reads "Wishing you and your family a New Year of peace, joy, and prosperity." The ad is actually an acknowledgement of the Jewish New Year, Rosh Hashana. The horn is called a Shofar and is typically blown during this time of celebration.

Shared reading prompts

Show the ad to the students. Ask them to consider both the visual images and the text to try to make sense of the message. Explain that even if they don't know what the ad is about, they can use their background knowledge to infer some possible reasons for the ad. Prompt them with some of the following questions:

- *Why would the company want to wish its customers a Happy New Year in September?*
- *What could the horn represent or symbolize?*
- *Is this ad designed for a wide audience or a specific group? Why?*
- *Does anyone have background knowledge of cultures with different holidays or calendars? How could that help us make sense of the ad?*
- *How does background knowledge help you interpret visual images?*
- *How can this experience help you interpret other ads more critically?*

- *What does this mean? What kinds of people stand out from the crowd? Why would someone want to stand out?*

- *Why are these creatures nondescript? What is the "personality" of the one who stands out? What can you infer from his look or attitude? What is the artist saying about members of the "crowd"?*

- *What is this an ad for? Who is the target audience? Why doesn't the advertiser make it clearer?*

Reading visual features

As with text features in general, the plethora and variety of visual features that students will find in texts (in print as well as electronic media) can be demystified and studied by using a shared reading approach followed by smaller group instruction and independent work. Some examples of features to use include:

- illustrations;
- tables, charts, and graphs;
- maps, including the use of keys;
- diagrams, including exploded diagrams, close-ups, and cross sections;
- photographs;
- flowcharts;
- timelines.

Information from visual images

Bill wanted to teach his students that they could make predictions, infer information, or gain additional meaning from visual images as well as from written texts. He started by using a classic black-and-white photograph in a shared reading lesson. The photograph featured a small boy in short pants and suspenders running down a street with a loaf of French bread under his arm. Bill modeled the inferences he could make. (The photograph was not set in the present. The photograph was taken in France.) He then asked the students to place the photograph in the context of a story.

- Why is he running away?
- What might have happened before the photograph was taken? What might happen next?
- Who is he? What kind of person is he?
- What is he thinking as he runs?

Some of his students responded in writing to this lesson, although this was not the primary objective of the lesson.

Help me. I just stole some bread from the baker. My name is James.
"I'll get you for that, James."
I better run away from the baker. I better eat it all up now before my Mom finds out. I'm going to eat my bread. I should take some home for my dog. I'll take him some now. How am I going to get past my Mom? I'm going to run home now.

By Alex

In a subsequent shared reading lesson, Bill used several photographs to model the various ways that they could convey information and to give his students opportunities to practice finding the information.

- *What can you learn about the setting of the story from this photograph?*
- *Do you think the women in the photograph live there? Why?/Why not?*
- *What else can you infer about the setting – the climate, the time of day, the place they are sitting? What is the story likely to be about?*
- *Who do you think it is written for?*

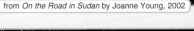

from *On the Road in Sudan* by Joanne Young, 2002

from *Lost in the Dark* by Sharon Hill, 2003

- *Who could these people be?*
- *Where are they? (country, area, climate, time)*
- *What can you infer from their clothing and from what they are doing?*
- *What's the story likely to be about?*

Teaching skills for research

In the process of reading to carry out research, students need to develop reliable research skills. These skills are best learned in the context of a real research project or inquiry – preferably one based on their own research interests. Shared reading can be used to introduce or reinforce the use of these skills. In the following example, the teacher uses a graphic organizer as a further scaffold for research.

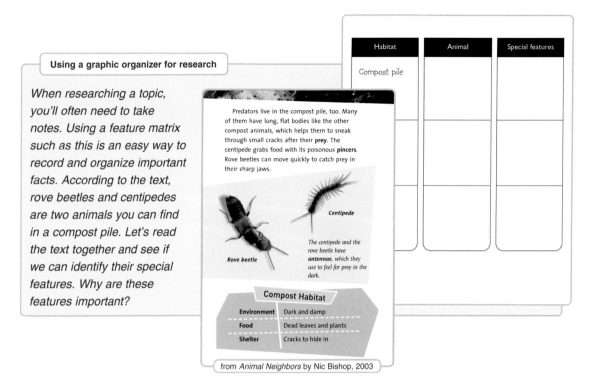

Using a graphic organizer for research

When researching a topic, you'll often need to take notes. Using a feature matrix such as this is an easy way to record and organize important facts. According to the text, rove beetles and centipedes are two animals you can find in a compost pile. Let's read the text together and see if we can identify their special features. Why are these features important?

Predators live in the compost pile, too. Many of them have long, flat bodies like the other compost animals, which helps them to sneak through small cracks after their **prey**. The centipede grabs food with its poisonous **pincers**. Rove beetles can move quickly to catch prey in their sharp jaws.

Centipede

Rove beetle

*The centipede and the rove beetle have **antennae**, which they use to feel for prey in the dark.*

Compost Habitat

Environment	Dark and damp
Food	Dead leaves and plants
Shelter	Cracks to hide in

Habitat	Animal	Special features
Compost pile		

from *Animal Neighbors* by Nic Bishop, 2003

Shared reading allows the teacher to model how to use skills for research and to encourage the students to demonstrate their use.

Other skills that can be modeled in shared reading and used for research include:

- skimming and scanning;
- distinguishing between relevant and irrelevant details;
- library skills (for example, how to use electronic and card catalogues);
- using keywords and phrases;
- summarizing information;
- categorizing information;
- taking notes;
- distinguishing between facts and opinions;
- synthesizing information from two or more sources;
- identifying author or cultural bias;
- comparing and contrasting information.

Teaching Internet reading

The Internet makes a vast amount of information available to anyone at any time. Many students are far more familiar and comfortable with the Internet than their teachers. It is a medium that presents some real challenges as well as exciting possibilities and opportunities. If teachers have access to the technology, they can display Web pages directly from the Internet via a data projector. Alternatively, they can print and enlarge Web pages to use in shared reading. Possible teaching objectives include:

- reading Web pages;

- using search engines (smart searching, using keywords, making choices from search results);

- using databases;

- navigating;

- critically analyzing and evaluating information;

- identifying bias;

- verifying or authenticating information; "Is this information true? How could we check it?"

- interpreting, summarizing, and presenting information.

from www.orbitforkids.com

Navigating or reading Web pages

– *How do I get back to the home page?*

– *Where do I go if I want to learn more about skating?*

– *Where do I click to find out more about risers?*

> **Using student-friendly search engines like Yahooligans**
>
> Reading the home page:
>
> - *Let's say you wanted to research the number of volcanoes that have erupted in the last one hundred years. Where would you go to find out the information? What keywords would you use?*
> - *Your favorite basketball team has just won an important game. Where would you go to find out who scored the winning basket?*
> - *You have to write a journal entry for current events. What image on this page tells you where to get more information?*
> - *Why does the engine use some graphics and some photos? Do they represent different kinds of information? How?*
> - *How do the icons make the page easier to navigate?*
> - *Where do you go if you get stuck and can't find what you're looking for?*
>
> Identifying bias on Web pages:
>
> - *Some icons are labeled as advertisements. Why is that? What do you think would happen if you clicked on them?*
> - *What are the items around the edge of the page? Why are they included?*
> - *What image captures your eye first? Why have they given this image the most importance?*
> - *What elements on this page are designed to get you to come back to the page on a regular basis? Why?*
> - *What audience is this page designed for? Which groups are they trying to target? (Consider age, economic background, interests, ethnicity.) How can you tell?*
> - *How could they make this page more useful for research projects?*
> - *In what ways are they advertising or promoting their own site?*

Teaching students to evaluate texts

In an age that has seen the proliferation of new forms of information, such as the Internet, television docudramas, and "faction" books, which combine facts with made-up information, it is no longer easy to distinguish fact from fiction. For example, historical fiction texts are a useful way of providing information about another place and time, but the reader has to learn how to discern between the facts and the storyline. Nonfiction is an extremely broad and ill-defined category, but one that most people associate with texts that are factual or "true." However, the veracity or authority of texts that appear to be nonfiction is no longer guaranteed. Multigenre texts that combine a variety of forms of fiction and nonfiction are becoming more common in classrooms and are also becoming more complex.

Given this explosion of information, it has become increasingly urgent that readers know another way of reading – one that is beyond the mechanics and the uses of reading for information and enjoyment. Students need to be taught to evaluate and question as they read. This is true for fiction as well as nonfiction texts.

By using shared reading as one approach in a repertoire of instructional strategies and approaches, the teacher can model the critical thinking that a reader must employ to sift fact from opinion, to recognize bias, and to uncover the position of the writer. Under the name of critical literacy (for example, Luke and Freebody, 1997), this kind of instruction is becoming increasingly common in schools around the world.

Short texts appropriate for shared reading can often be found in newspapers, magazines, posters, and material aimed specifically at young people. Some of these texts may be large enough to use for shared reading as they are. Others may need to be enlarged or transferred onto an overhead transparency. Full-page advertisements are a wonderful source, as are the sports headlines. Texts must have relevance and meaning to the students to give them a starting point from which to critique the texts.

Judging a book by its cover

A form of text evaluation that can expand the independent reading repertoires of students is the use of back cover blurbs in shared reading. In the following example, a teacher shares her own strategies for choosing a new novel to read. She then uses the blurbs from several novels for young people in order to show her students how they can evaluate and select novels for their own reading.

Strategies for choosing a novel

Finding the right book is something I take very seriously. I don't want to waste time reading a book that won't interest me. To help me choose, I always read the blurb on the back of the book, and the quotes from reviews. Then I ask myself a series of questions:

- *Who's the author? What else have they written?*
- *Have I ever heard anyone talk about this author or title?*
- *Who reviewed the book? Are they respected book critics?*
- *Do the reviews reveal anything interesting about the book? Does it sound similar to books I've liked in the past?*
- *Where is the story set?*
- *What is the genre? (There are genres I like and others I don't like.)*
- *Does the blurb make me think about anything from my own life? Will I be able to relate to the story?*
- *Who's the main character in the story? Will I like them? Will I care what happens to them?*
- *Is the book part of a series? If I like it, will there be others to follow?*

Now look at these examples from books written for your age level. We'll read the blurb together and then try asking some similar questions.

- *"Ish the Traveler" sounds unusual to me. Is it a fantasy story, or does it just take place in a foreign land?*
- *When and where do you think the story takes place?*
- *The blurb describes this as a "universal" story. What does that mean?*
- *The blurb mentions Shaman, mysteries, and a dark and menacing presence ... What do these words tell you about the mood of the book?*
- *Look at the cover. How do the images add to the mysterious qualities of the story? What do they make you think about?*
- *What's the "hook?" What kind of story do you think this will be?*

We must trust everyone and no one.

In the harsh land of the Great White Bear, Ish the Traveler finds a rescuer and a companion – the Bear Man. Through their friendship Ish discovers the Bear Man is a servant of the village people; their wise one, their healer, their Shaman.

In this timeless, universal story Ish gains wisdom and a place. He learns the profound power of knowledge, the terrifying force of superstition, and witnesses first hand the mysteries of the human spirit. But in this land of blinding light there lurks a dark, menacing presence threatening all who may offend her.

from *The Shaman and the Droll* by Jack Lasenby, 1999

46

If it is your intention to knock me on the head, boy, kindly get it over and done with. If it is robbery you're bent on, I might as well warn you the pickings will be slim, scarce worth your effort ...

There are two sides to Damon. You can see it in his face – Good Face, Bad Face. Which is the true Damon? The one who hits first and asks questions later? Or the one who acts out of kindness?

When the mysterious Esther enters his life, Damon finds his mask beginning to slip. And even he doesn't know what he'll find behind it.

Good Face. Bad Face. Good Face. Bad Face. Same Face? One Face?

from *Scarface and the Angel* by William Taylor, 2000

– Before we read anything, let's look at the images on the cover.

– What do you notice about the images? What do they evoke?

– Think about the title. Does it sound familiar? Does it grab your attention?

– Let's read the text on the back. Who do you think is talking at first?

– How can there be two sides to one person? What kind of story does this hint at?

– Esther is described as mysterious. What role do you think she'll play in the story?

– The blurb ends with a riddle. Does it make you want to read on?

– How does the blurb grab your attention? Does it work?

– What does the "conversational style" tell you about the book?

– Why does the narrator refer to other characters as amoebae? What does this imply?

– Have you ever made prank phone calls? How could they lead to murder?

– The blurb mentions love and humor as well as mystery and death. How can these different ideas be combined successfully? Does this intrigue you?

– Four million copies of this book have been sold. What does that tell you about the book?

– What does "Pulitzer prizewinner" mean?

I suppose it all started when Lorraine and I and these two amoebae called Dennis and Norton were hot on these phone gags last September. We made up a new game in which the main object was to keep a stranger talking on the phone for as long as possible. ... Now Lorraine can blame all the other things on me, but she was the one who picked out the Pigman's phone number. If you ask me, I think he would have died anyway. Maybe we speeded things up a little, but you can't really say we murdered him. Not murdered him.

Written by a Pulitzer prizewinner, this dramatic story that unfolds in the diary confessions of two young lovers, has sold over 4,000,000 copies worldwide.

from *The Pigman* by Paul Zindel, 1968

Finding texts for shared reading: they're everywhere!

Shared reading gives teachers a wonderful opportunity to be creative in their selection and use of texts. Multiple copies are unnecessary, enlargement is not difficult, and once the search for suitable texts has begun, they appear in all kinds of unusual places.

Note that making copies of copyright materials without permission may be illegal. Check with the publisher, the local authorities, or the copyright holder to find out whether you can reproduce materials for teaching purposes.

Identifying point of view

PLAINVILLE NEWS

Dog attacks cat and must leave town!

Mac the dog attacked a cat called Misty yesterday. The local council says that Mac must leave town because he's too dangerous. Mac's owner and neighbors on West Street think he should stay!

Misty and her owner

Our class got into two groups. One group had to write about why Mac should stay and the other group about why Mac should leave.

Group 1: Mac should stay	Group 2: Mac should leave
• Mac hasn't hurt any other cats before, so he probably won't do it again.	• Mac should be punished for hurting the cat.
• His owner should have taken better care of him so that he didn't hurt the cat. The owner should be punished, not Mac.	• His owner hasn't taken good care of him, so Mac should go to a new home.
• The cat was hurt, but now she's better.	• He might do it again, so he should be kept away from cats.
• Dogs are usually friendly. Mac probably didn't mean to attack the cat.	• If he attacked my cat, I'd be very upset.
• The cat might have teased Mac.	• That's what the council rules say.
	• My dad says that Mac should leave Plainville because he's dangerous.

from *Should Mac Leave Town?* by Sharon Hill, 2001

The key to finding texts to use for shared reading is choosing the right text for the job. For example:

- To help students become better at identifying a point of view, select a text in which the writer has developed a sound argument leading to a point of view. A good example of a third grade text that explores two points of view with supporting arguments is *Should Mac Leave Town?* (Hill, 2001).

- To provide practice at working out the meanings of unfamiliar words in context, select a text that has some challenging words with a strong supporting context.

- To show students how they can increase understanding by cross-checking textual with graphic information, select a page from an early reader and one from a nonfiction text that challenged them.

Cross-checking information

When you were younger and you were just learning to read, you frequently relied on the illustrations in a text to help you figure out the meaning. Look at this piece of text from the book In the Dark Forest. *The illustration provides more detail, so young readers can use it to really get a picture of what the words tell you.*

Lizard comes out.

from *In the Dark Forest* by Karrin Mahuika, 1997

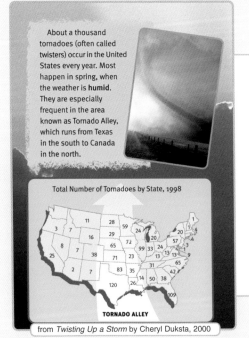

About a thousand tornadoes (often called twisters) occur in the United States every year. Most happen in spring, when the weather is **humid**. They are especially frequent in the area known as Tornado Alley, which runs from Texas in the south to Canada in the north.

Total Number of Tornadoes by State, 1998

TORNADO ALLEY

from *Twisting Up a Storm* by Cheryl Duksta, 2000

Now look at this example from a book we used in our weather unit. As fluent readers, you can still use the visual cues to help you make meaning of the text. "Tornado Alley" may be a new phrase for you. The text says that it runs from Texas to Canada, but you would have to know your geography pretty well to be able to picture it. The graphic helps you confirm your understanding of the text and provides more detail. Just as you used cross-checking between the words and the pictures as a new reader, you can use the visual cues, the graphics, and the text to help you figure out complicated ideas and new vocabulary.

49

Further suggestions for shared reading texts include:

- short stories;
- large picture books;
- extracts from novels;
- menus;
- recipes or experiments;
- articles, including those from newspapers and magazines;
- schedules, tickets, and programs;
- advertisements – even a nearby billboard;
- visual texts, such as photographs and diagrams;
- textbook pages;
- practice tests;
- directions and other procedural texts.

CHAPTER 4

Assessment-driven Instruction

Shared reading is a terrific informal assessment tool because through discussion you know where your students are, and you know what they're thinking. You can ask other students during the shared reading lesson "Who else is thinking that way?", and if it's not something you can deal with right then, you make a note of it and bring those students together later for clarification, maybe in a guided reading group.

Mary, grade 5 teacher

Assessment and teaching

Assessment is an integral part of teaching and learning, and it takes many forms. To be most useful, the assessment information should be gathered directly from the students and should show their strengths and their learning needs. This data is then used to inform planning. Within the planning process, decisions are made about the learning objectives, the best approaches to use, and the materials that will be needed. Once the teaching has been carried out, the students' progress is reviewed as part of the ongoing assessment that continues to inform planning. In this way, assessment drives instruction.

Informal assessment

During reading conferences, Tim noticed that several of his students found it difficult to make sense of stories that contained a lot of dialogue. They were not always clear who was doing the talking. Because of this, the students weren't able to link characters to actions, and so meaning was lost. Over the next week, Tim made a point of observing and listening to his students as they read and discussed stories with dialogue. His observations showed that many students became confused when reading more complex dialogue. It became clear that students were not self-monitoring for meaning. Because this was a widespread problem, he decided to address it by using a shared reading approach and an extract from a book with good examples of complex dialogue. The way Tim addressed this problem is discussed on page 57.

In the same way as any other instruction, shared reading needs to be planned and based on assessment. A great deal of information can also be gathered *during* a shared reading lesson. Students' responses, their contributions to discussions, and their observations about a text all give the teacher valuable information about their levels of comprehension and their ability to use the strategies being taught.

In the interactive environment of a shared reading lesson, teachers can also observe how well their students engage with each other. This is more than a social concern. The teacher needs to know about their students' ability and willingness to participate in the kind of talk that develops group and individual learning. Assessment of these aspects of a lesson can drive future teaching decisions. For example, a few lessons may need to be devoted to the mechanics of giving and receiving feedback within a group setting.

Knowing the learners

Effective teachers are constantly observing and monitoring their students' reading behavior, as Tim did in the example above, and using their observations to inform their teaching decisions. This "student watching" is one of the most important forms of assessment that teachers can use as they plan and review their teaching.

As students in grade 3 and beyond gain confidence in reading, teachers will be noting behaviors such as:

- reading fluency;

- relating their own experiences to texts;

- making, confirming, and revising predictions;

- self-monitoring for sense and accuracy;

- reading between the lines or inferring meaning;

- identifying an author's point of view;

- using nonfiction features effectively;

- working out the meanings of new or unfamiliar words from context;

- noticing literary and language devices;

- distinguishing fact from opinion;

- determining important details;

- synthesizing information;

- drawing conclusions.

With older students, teachers still need to monitor and, in many cases, actually teach the above behaviors. Teachers also need to look for more sophisticated uses of reading. Some behaviors they could note include:

- reading critically to determine an author's purpose, point of view, and possible bias;

- making and comparing interpretations of texts;

- integrating strategies as they read (evidenced by seamless monitoring and mending as they read);

- using evidence in the text to support their assertions;

- evaluating fiction and nonfiction texts according to criteria;

- searching for, selecting, categorizing, and synthesizing information;

- comparing and using information presented in different formats;

- making personal responses to texts in ways that reflect a depth of analysis and an ability to connect the text with their own knowledge of the world.

If teachers assume knowledge or skills that the students do not yet possess, the students will become frustrated, switch off, and see themselves as failures. If, on the other hand, teachers do not recognize the learning the students already have, the students may become bored and achieve less than they are able to. By identifying what their students can do, teachers can set a starting point from which to build new learning. This information can show what needs to be reinforced and what needs to be modeled and taught. It will also make the links to new learning more explicit for the students.

Sources of assessment information

Opportunities to assess what students can do include:

- conferences and observations during independent reading time;

- observations of students during shared, guided, and other instructional reading sessions;

- direct discussion with students about their reading preferences and problems;

- self-assessment (where students assess their own performance against clearly defined criteria);

- analysis of draft writing pieces;

- individual writing conferences;

- student surveys;

- analysis of running records or other informal diagnostic procedures (may be most appropriate for struggling readers);

- analysis of the results of formal (often standardized) tests.

Putting the information together

Assessment provides valuable information about individual students, but teachers often have difficulty applying the information about individual students to the class or to groups within the class. The time spent transferring data about individual students onto a class summary sheet is repaid when decisions need to be made about grouping for small-group instruction or about the objectives for whole-class instruction, such as a shared reading lesson.

Ricardo, a grade 4 teacher in Brooklyn, New York, summarized the information he had gathered from his students into a chart:

Class Summary Sheet *Mr. Alvarez*   Grade 4

Name	Date	Instructional Needs
Chastity	4/18	Learn how to identify features of different genres and use them to help understand texts. Develop broader reading interests. Confidently participate in group discussion by building on what others have said.
Matthew	4/16	Pause and reread to increase self-monitoring. Improve fluency by using punctuation and phrases. Read more deeply — make inferences about characters' actions and feelings.
Ali	4/15	Increase confidence in small-group discussion. Use text as a support, including syntax clues: Does this sound right? Reread to improve fluency and meaning.
Elizabeth	4/15	Improve self-monitoring by rereading and skimming and scanning previous pages. Decodes well but needs to make connections with knowledge of story schema and character relationships. Actively question during reading to establish connections.
Jose	4/15	Use syntax clues: Does it sound right? Increase fluency by adding expression to enhance meaning. Infer using text and genre features.
Aurelyn	4/19	Improve self-monitoring by actively asking questions and making connections during reading. Build confidence in small- and large-group discussion. Skim and scan text to make more purposeful predictions.
Saleb	4/19	Monitor for sense and reread if meaning is lost. Increase fluency and expression, especially when dialogue is in text. Read ahead to identify punctuation and phrasing to help fluency. Read through whole word using suffixes to identify unknown words.
Adriana	4/19	Improve self-monitoring, asking question: Does this make sense? Learn how to make appropriate independent reading choices. Use context clues to solve unknown words and known chunks of words. Use knowledge of series to help make meaning of further books.
Jason	4/19	Reread to establish meaning. Use knowledge of story schema to help make predictions during the reading. Use context clues to solve unknown words. Identify relevant and important details.
Angel	4/22	Activate and use prior knowledge to help connect ideas during reading. Identify use of stereotypes and bias.

Most of Ricardo's students had a Spanish-speaking background and were able to decode well. However, many did not find reading English texts worthwhile or enjoyable. When Ricardo went back to the individual reading records, they revealed what he had already suspected: that many of his students could read aloud accurately but were not making sense of the texts they read. They were not monitoring for sense so were not aware when meaning was lost. Despite their reading accuracy, many of these students did not read fluently and lacked confidence in their reading ability. Several of his students failed to use what they already knew about how texts work or failed to make connections with the text. This greatly reduced their ability to make meaning. By looking at the data for his class as a whole, Ricardo was able to make decisions about appropriate teaching objectives.

For shared reading with the whole class, Ricardo initially decided on these objectives:

- use prior knowledge by connecting what they know with the text;

- monitor for sense by asking questions about the text;

- use punctuation and phrases to increase fluency.

He chose these reading strategies to focus on because he felt that they would support his students in moving on and experiencing some success in their reading. Later, he would be able to add more strategies and increase their ability to delve more deeply into meaning.

Over several weeks, Ricardo carried out shared reading lessons on a variety of topics to which he knew his students could bring prior knowledge. He demonstrated the ways in which good readers anticipate meaning by thinking about their own knowledge or experience. He modeled ways that he could use his prior knowledge to help make meaning of the texts. In other lessons, he showed how good readers could reread, ask questions of the text, pause and reflect, or make personal connections when they didn't understand. He also showed how they could use context clues to work out new words. Through every lesson, he built his students' fluency by modeling good reading and explaining how he used the punctuation and phrases as he read aloud. He provided many opportunities for his students to practice rereading phrases and sentences aloud with him and in pairs during shared reading lessons. Ricardo monitored the learning by taking brief notes on his students during shared, guided, and independent reading. He also took running records of his most at-risk students so that he could follow their progress more closely.

Selecting objectives for shared reading based on assessment data

When selecting objectives or purposes for shared reading lessons, teachers should use the assessment information discussed above and keep these guiding questions in mind:

- *What do my students need to know or be able to do?* The answer may be based on such factors as the curriculum requirements or the teacher's knowledge of school expectations, the reading developmental process, and the teacher's knowledge of what the students can already do.

- *What skills, strategies, or abilities do they already have?* This information can be charted for individuals, groups, and the whole class.

- *What is the next logical, achievable step for them?* The objectives for individuals, groups, and the whole class can be charted.

- *Which approach will best meet the needs of the students?* If large numbers of students have a similar need, shared reading is an obvious choice.

- *How will I know when my students have improved? What evidence will I look for?* By planning the assessment of new learning in advance, teachers make themselves accountable for teaching and learning. An important aspect of this is telling the students what the expected outcomes will be. For example, the teacher could plan to record students' oral reading before and after several lessons aimed to improve fluency. The teacher and the students will be able to evaluate for themselves how successful the teaching and learning have been.

In the example on page 51, Tim identified reading dialogue as a problem for many of his students. Tim's objectives were for his students to:

- use clues and conventions in the text (speech marks, use of speakers' names) to identify speakers;

- learn how to monitor for meaning;

- reread when meaning is lost.

He would know that the objectives were being met when his students could read and understand a piece of complex dialogue and could explain how they maintained meaning with that dialogue.

Tim did not have to teach everything about dialogue because his students already had some knowledge of how it works. Building on what students can already do helps to establish links. It is also far easier to build on something that is familiar than something that is not.

Tracking complex dialogue

They were laughing and playing ball when Palmer, letting fly a long shot from beyond the bed, said, "Do you like my father?"

Dorothy watched the ball bounce off the door. "What kind of question is that?"

"Do you?"

"Sure, why?"

"Do you think he's nice?"

"Yeah, don't you?"

Palmer thought for a moment. "Yeah, he is. I guess that's the problem."

Dorothy rolled her eyes. "You're talking goofy. What problem?"

"The golden bird."

Dorothy threw the ball at him. "Will you please make some sense?"

from *Wringer* by Jerry Spinelli, 1997

Tim copied an extract from a text that his students had struggled with and reproduced it on an overhead transparency for a shared reading lesson. His purpose was to find out more about what his students were doing when they encountered dialogue and to show them how to use what they already knew about dialogue. Before reading the extract to the group, he explained that good readers notice when their reading stops making sense. He told them that he had noticed many students getting lost when they read a long piece of dialogue and that today's lesson would focus on ways to fix up their reading when they became confused. Tim discussed the things that his students already knew about reading dialogue in order to prepare them to make connections with new learning. He then asked his students to raise their hands as he read the passage aloud if they weren't sure which character was speaking. After reading the text through once, Tim returned to the points at which hands had started to go up. He probed for suggestions:

– *What happened for you at this point?*
– *What could you have done to find out who was speaking?*
– *How can you keep tabs on these speakers?*

Tim used the students' suggestions, such as those of rereading, writing names beside the dialogue, reading with a different voice for each person, and reading the text through again. On Tim's second reading, very few hands went up. Tim checked for the students' use of strategies:

> – *How do writers usually tell us who is speaking?*
> – *What can we do when they don't give us these clues?*

Tim discussed and, where appropriate, modeled how the students could use a combination of strategies (monitoring for sense by stopping and rereading when they lost track or using dialogue markers) to maintain the meaning of dialogue in a story. Over the next two weeks, he used three more examples of dialogue in shared reading lessons to allow his students to practice these strategies. He also selected texts for his guided reading groups that used dialogue. Over the next weeks, he monitored how well his students had learned and applied the strategies, and he continued to help those who were not confident. In this example, the teacher used shared reading to:

- assess (by finding out exactly where his students lost meaning);

- teach strategies (by modeling and giving opportunities for practice);

- evaluate learning (by monitoring the use of the strategies in subsequent lessons and in other reading situations).

CHAPTER 5

The Shared Reading Lesson

Elements of a shared reading lesson

Every shared reading lesson is different. The purpose, the familiarity of the text, and the levels of support needed all vary greatly. Shared reading is not a spontaneous event: it is intentional, planned, and purposeful. Successful implementation depends on being well organized with the appropriate materials and tools in place. The following description assumes that assessment of needs, selection of objectives and an appropriate text, and planning of key questions have already taken place.

Introducing the text

This stage of the lesson is important for motivating the students and generating their interest in the reading. A common and powerful way to do this is by connecting with the students' prior knowledge about a topic or a text type. Eliciting prior knowledge should not only generate the students' interest but also alert them to think about what they already know. It "activates their schema" and prepares them for the learning to come. If the topic is outside their experience or knowledge, the teacher should spend time on building background, for example, by using artifacts, photographs, or stories on which to ground the shared reading text. This process may take a few minutes. However, if the topic is important and the students have nothing in their own lives to enable them to make connections, the teacher may wish to spend more time, possibly over several days, building up enough knowledge for the focus text or topic to have meaning.

The teacher may explain to the students why the text was chosen, what the purpose of the lesson is, or both. Such explanation is more meaningful if the teacher can link it to the students' needs. The introduction may include setting focus questions that will be used during the lesson. The teacher can plan these in advance or decide on them with the class. There are many ways to start a shared reading lesson. But whatever way the teacher decides to introduce the lesson, this stage should be kept brief and focused.

Reading and discussing the text – the teacher's role

1. Reading the text aloud

No matter what the teacher's purpose for conducting a shared reading lesson, engaging the students' interest and heightening their motivation to make meaning should be paramount. Such engagement is not an easy matter, particularly as the students move toward adolescence, but a lively, engaging reading style helps to achieve it.

- In the first reading of a new text, the teacher often reads aloud as the students follow with their eyes.

- The teacher will have read the text before the lesson so that she or he can model fluent, expressive reading.

- In general, but by no means in all cases, the first reading of a new text is done with a minimal amount of pause or interruption. This gives the students an overview of the piece and will help them to make meaning.

- Later rereadings may be broken up with such practices as questions and discussion, thinking aloud by the teacher or students, clarification of specific parts of the text, and word work.

- The amount of pausing during reading varies according to the type of text and the needs of the students. For example, if the purpose is to study the features of a labeled diagram, the teacher may wish to read and discuss each label in turn.

- After the first reading, the teacher may go back and read all or part of the text aloud and invite the students to participate in the reading. This practice helps to focus the students on the text, requires them to become actively involved, and continues to develop their fluency skills.

- The teacher may the invite students to join in by pausing at certain places and allowing them to complete a phrase or sentence.

- The teacher may use a pointer to help focus the students on the text.

2. Explicit instruction

During the reading and discussion of the text, the teacher provides explicit instruction based on the purposes of the lesson. This may involve modeling the use of a particular strategy or telling the students how to read a specific form of text for a specific purpose. Some of these forms of explicit instruction are included below, and others are described in chapters 6, 7, 8, and 9.

- The teacher models how an expert reader would read or interpret the text according to the purpose that has been set. This modeling may involve thinking aloud, making notes on a whiteboard, or rereading parts of the text.

- If a specific strategy is being taught or if the focus is on integrating the use of several strategies, the teacher models how she or he uses these strategies.

- The teacher monitors for engagement to ensure that the students are actively listening. If the attention of all or part of the group wanders, the modeling will be ineffective.

- The teacher may also model how to build on the responses of others and how to ask questions based on these responses. This promotes "accountable talk" and more critical thinking in the class.

Modeling

Yesterday I showed you how I monitor my understanding as I read, making adjustments as I go. Good readers notice when they are making meaning and when they need to do something to fix their confusion. When I find myself getting confused, the first thing I do is reread the tricky part. If I'm still stuck, I start to ask questions of the text, the author, or myself. For example, I ask myself, "What do I need to know in order to make sense of this text?" If I don't have enough prior knowledge, I consider where I might go to find out more. Many times, all I have to do is look up a word or two in the dictionary or ask someone who knows more about the topic. Other times, questioning the text or considering the author's purpose works better to clear up my confusion.

When I pause to ask these kinds of questions, it slows me down as a reader, but it helps me focus on exactly where I got confused. The trick is stopping myself as soon as I notice that the text is no longer making sense. Being aware of your confusion will help you enormously when you are reading complicated passages from textbooks or novels. Let's look at this page from your science text on the overhead. I'll model how I fix up my confusion in the first paragraph, and then you can help me out with the rest of the page.

---

3. Encouraging active engagement

In shared reading, the text itself and the purpose of the lesson influence the discussion that occurs. Chapter 7 outlines ways in which careful questioning, prompting, and feedback can lead to deeper understanding of texts. The teacher's ability to actively engage the students in reading and discussing the text is critical in shared reading.

- If this is a first lesson with a specific text, the teacher does more of the talking as they show students how to work it out. As the students become more confident, the teacher encourages them to take more responsibility for working it out together, supporting and leading them to do it by themselves or in pairs.

- To promote discussion, the teacher uses planned questions or discussion starters linked to the lesson's purpose and the students' interests and experiences.

- The teacher may encourage the students to reread parts of the text aloud but never as a test of reading ability. Students can, for example, read key sentences, phrases, or labels for diagrams to allow them to participate actively rather than passively.

- Questions need to challenge the students and should provide models that they can use themselves.

- The teacher needs to constantly be careful not to place students in high-risk situations when encouraging their participation.

- Maintaining eye contact with the students, including those sitting at the outer edges of the group, helps to involve everyone in the lesson. Students culturally unaccustomed to direct eye contact with adults can be encouraged to participate in other ways, such as by physical proximity or direct prompts.

- The teacher's feedback on student responses should scaffold the learning, for example, by prompting further thinking, clarifying a point, or confirming. Feedback can and should come from the students too as they support each other's learning. See chapter 7.

- It is helpful to have a whiteboard or chart paper nearby to record aspects of the discussion, to chart or record structural features of the text discussed, or to explore unfamiliar vocabulary.

- The teacher should encourage discussion between the students. For example, the teacher may direct the students to discuss a specific point in pairs (this may be a regular pairing or simply two students who sit next to each other) or may use small groupings for brief discussions before they report back to the larger group to share ideas.

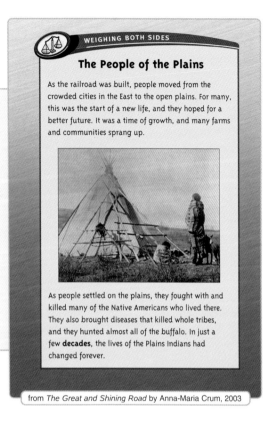

Encouraging discussion during the lesson

We've been reading a lot about the movement of people to the West and the difficulties they encountered. Read this text with me, then turn to a partner and talk about the information here.

- *How does it compare with what we've read before?*
- *Is there any new information here?*

Right, now I want you to think about the heading at the top – Weighing Both Sides. With your partner, decide what those sides could be. Take one side each and state your case. We'll share these in a few minutes.

WEIGHING BOTH SIDES

The People of the Plains

As the railroad was built, people moved from the crowded cities in the East to the open plains. For many, this was the start of a new life, and they hoped for a better future. It was a time of growth, and many farms and communities sprang up.

As people settled on the plains, they fought with and killed many of the Native Americans who lived there. They also brought diseases that killed whole tribes, and they hunted almost all of the buffalo. In just a few **decades**, the lives of the Plains Indians had changed forever.

from *The Great and Shining Road* by Anna-Maria Crum, 2003

Reading and discussing the text – the students' role

When I use shared reading with social studies texts, it gives the kids an opportunity to pick apart a complex text with a group of people rather than sitting with a text alone, which at times can be extremely difficult. I act as a guide, I give them a focus, and I show them how I'd go about reading the text. Then I give them an opportunity to bounce ideas off of one another, to ask questions, to feel validated. Shared reading gives them an opportunity to turn and talk, to think on their own but to think with me and the text right there, and to feel supported.

Elizabeth, grade 5 teacher

A shared reading lesson is an instructional time, and the students should know what is expected of them. The introduction will have provided them with the focus for the lesson and oriented them to the text.

- All eyes need to be on the text, and the students need to know that the teacher expects them to read along silently or aloud and to be listening carefully.

- The students need to think about the text by relating it to what they already know about the topic or about similar kinds of texts. They should be encouraged to use the strategies they are already familiar with, such as making connections, predicting, and visualizing.

- Following the teacher's example, the students should be reflecting on their own thinking and adapting or incorporating new ways of thinking. The teacher should carefully foster this metacognitive activity, reminding the students of it as they read, listen, and participate in the discussion.

- Shared reading is a time for trying out the strategy or kind of reading that is being taught. The students need to be prepared to "have a go" even when they are not sure they are right. They can try the process out in pairs or small groups before the discussion is shared with the larger group. The time and focus need to be carefully managed to prevent the discussion from becoming off-task chatting.

- The students need to know that they are expected to ask and respond to questions and prompts, to listen to others, and to build on others' responses.

- If the teacher has requested hand raising, note taking, or other actions, the students need to have any materials ready and to carry out these actions when appropriate.

- The students must observe their usual classroom management rules such as showing others respect, not talking over others, and taking turns.

- If shared reading interactions don't happen naturally, they can be taught through modeling, rehearsing, or splitting the group to involve some students in the shared reading discussion while others observe. It may be more appropriate to teach these habits of interaction in separate mini-lessons.

For example, if a student says the same thing as another student, I might interject and say "Oh, then you agree with what Susie said," so that you begin to socialize with that language and get that language out there. Again, it's modeling. It's describing and modeling to the kids how we should speak to one another.

Miles, grade 4 teacher

After the reading – following up

Shared reading lessons often build on each other, and it is unusual for a single lesson to cover a teaching objective to the point where the students can apply the learning independently. For this reason, the best follow-up to a shared reading lesson may well be another lesson using the same text or a different text with the same purpose on a later day. The degree of teacher support (for example, the amount of modeling used) will decrease as the students master the strategy being taught.

Other forms of follow-up allow the students to practice what they have learned. Not all students will be able to apply new learning after the shared reading lesson, which is why it needs to be followed up. Such follow-up work could be completed in smaller groups, in independent practice, or in other parts of the literacy program. The reduced support and closer teacher–student focus available in guided reading may be the best form of following up for many students. In guided reading, students can practice and demonstrate strategies already taught in shared reading.

Shared reading opens up many options for follow-up work. For example, if the purpose of the shared reading lesson is to explore the figurative language in a poem, follow-up activities could include:

City Song

There's a forest of buildings
in place of the trees,
and the birds have all flown
with the wind in the leaves.

Replacing their song
is the tune of the city –
the hum of the traffic
and the rustle of litter.

There is energy here
and it's fast and it's bright
the stores and the movies
are open all night.

That haze in the sky, though,
isn't cloud but bad air
that makes your eyes water
and dirties your hair.

And, just think, when night comes
and the sun sinks down low
in place of the stars
the neon signs glow.

Jenny Bornholdt, 2002

- focusing more closely on the poem in a guided reading lesson (on the same or a later day, depending on the students' needs);

- analyzing, individually or in small groups, the language used in two or three similar poems;

- returning to the poem studied and, either independently or in pairs, recording the examples of figurative language and their effects in the poem;

- developing their poetic writing by adding figurative language to simple descriptions – as a teacher-led shared writing activity, or in small groups, or individually;

- using the language studied to co-write a poem in a group;

- identifying and discussing the use of metaphor in this and other poems to explain or describe phenomena in nature;

- exploring the use of figurative language in nonfiction texts, for example, in textbook descriptions of meteorological features.

The follow-up activity can happen immediately or later that day or week. It can occur in a variety of ways and in many parts of the program. However, it is not essential for every shared reading lesson to have a follow-up. As always, it depends on the needs of the students.

For a closer exploration of the links between shared reading and the writing process, see chapter 10.

CHAPTER 6

Showing How: Explaining and Modeling

An important reason for using shared reading beyond the first few years of school is to improve the quality and depth of students' thinking. In particular, shared reading facilitates teaching comprehension strategies because it allows for explicit instruction. For example, the teacher can model the strategy being taught and use prompting to shape the students' responses as they learn to carry out the same kind of thinking for themselves.

Discussions that promote learning can follow on from this modeling. The teacher's use of careful questioning, prompting, and feedback encourages the talk to continue and build. This chapter explores explaining and modeling in shared reading, and chapter 7 examines questioning and feedback.

Telling and explaining

Most people can remember resisting doing something because they saw no reason for it. "Because I said so" may be the only reason given for a lot of tedious tasks that children are asked to do. Sometimes that's a good enough explanation. If, however, children are expected to learn from the task, it helps them to know *why* they are doing it. The difference between telling and explaining is that telling says *what* whereas explaining says *why*.

In teaching, it's important that the students know what they are about to learn and why it is important. In chapter 5, ways of introducing a shared reading lesson were described. The introduction can and usually should include the what and why of the lesson. This sets the purpose. Lengthy explanations turn students off, but it is important to alert them to the learning that they are expected to gain from the lesson.

Setting the purpose

Purpose 1

I've noticed that many of you are not going very deeply into the books you read. Today we're going to learn how making comparisons and using what we already know about a type of book can help us to predict what's in a text. When you can make predictions about the content of a book and compare it to similar books you've read before, you will be able to understand it better and get more out of the story. Think about a story you've read that described the life of a real person. These stories are called biographies. What things can you expect to find in a biography?

Purpose 2

Sometimes it's important to share a book, a passage, or a poem with someone simply because you really liked it. By sharing your enjoyment of the text, you'll create a connection between you and that person, get something new out of the piece by rereading it, and understand it on a deeper level. Today I'm going to share a poem I just read called "Rain" by Hone Tuwhare. We're all tired of having indoor recess, but after I read this poem I felt better about all the rain we've been having. Plus, I just wanted to share it aloud with someone because it sounds so beautiful.

Purpose 3

We're going to look at a page from chapter 4, which is about saving energy, and figure out what's the most important information. Readers who can identify the "big ideas" have an easier time remembering important facts, answering questions, and determining the author's purpose.

Rain

I can hear you making
small holes in the silence
rain

If I were deaf
the pores of my skin
would open to you
and shut

And I should know you
by the lick of you
if I were blind:

the steady drum-roll
sound you make
when the wind drops

the something
special smell of you
when the sun cakes
the ground

But if I should not
hear
smell or feel or see you

you would still
define me
disperse me
wash over me
rain

Hone Tuwhare, 1964

Modeling

As discussed earlier, shared reading is an excellent approach to use for scaffolding learning. Modeling is a powerful and effective way of providing this scaffolding.

If telling and explaining are the *what* and *why*, modeling is the *how*.

Within a shared reading lesson, a teacher can model how she or he approaches a new text or applies a specific comprehension strategy. The teacher does this by, for example, voicing thoughts, predictions, and questions about the text.

> **Modeling: Approaching a new text**
>
> *Nonfiction texts often describe things in the natural world and then explain why they happen. In this passage, the author described the causes of erosion. I'm going to use what I just learned and combine it with what I've seen in nature in order to infer what the effects of erosion might be. Here the author talks about wind. I'm picturing the dunes I've seen at the coast. I'm guessing they have many different shapes that change because they are being constantly eroded by the wind. And here where she talks about water, I'm picturing the cliffs near the river. I'm thinking they were caused by the water eroding the land and carving out the cliffs.*

One way that people can understand modeling is to think about times when they've learned something from an expert. Usually the expert is showing them how to do something concrete or physical: how to cook, how to perform an exercise in yoga, how to build a bookcase. Being shown is much more powerful than simply reading instructions or being told what to do.

The modeling used in shared reading is similar to these examples, but there is also a major difference. In shared reading, teachers are modeling things that happen inside the head. When teachers model in a shared reading lesson, they are teaching their students to be metacognitive in their reading by showing how they think about their own thinking. One of the most widely used forms of modeling is thinking out loud.

Thinking out loud

Sometimes referred to as "think-alouds," this teaching strategy or protocol (Pressley and Afflerbach, 1995; Wilhelm 2001) involves the teacher in talking about what is happening in her or his mind as they read a text. Of course, the teacher can't reproduce every single thought that passes through their mind. Thinking aloud for instructional purposes aims to show just enough to give the listener an idea of what's happening. Whatever is demonstrated through thinking aloud should be tied to the teaching objective.

Showing how by thinking aloud

Exploring literary devices

I wonder why the author starts this story with a description of stormy weather? I know that authors often use something called foreshadowing to hint at what will happen later in the story. I am thinking that the brewing storm is a hint by the author that something bad is going to happen.

Working out words

I'm confused by this word "cartography." I don't know what it means. I've seen the ending before in biography and photography. I'm going to use what I know about those words to help me figure the new word. A biography is the story of someone's life. Photography means to capture an image on film. Both are ways of recording something. I'm guessing that the root "graphy" means to record or document. The story is about a man who loved maps. I'm guessing that cartography means recording something in the form of a map.

Understanding a character

I'm wondering why the boy is nervous. But now I'm thinking about how I felt the first time I had to baby-sit. I was sure I was going to do something wrong or that something bad was going to happen to the baby. Now I understand why he's anxious about being left at home in charge of his little brother. When I can connect what's happening with the character to something that happened in my own life, I have a better understanding of what the character is feeling.

Wilhelm (2001) states that expert readers read automatically and may find it hard to articulate how they make meaning as they read. "[Think-alouds] make us slow down and take a look at our own reading processes. They show us what students are doing – and not doing – as they engage in the reading process, and they help students to take on our expert strategies" (page 27).

Showing how on the text

Although thinking out loud is usually done orally, there are other ways of modeling. The teacher can write on or mark the text to show the students how to use a strategy or to highlight features of the text. This is often done at the same time as thinking out loud. The aim is to make the thinking explicit by producing a model in written form.

Depending on the materials used, writing on the text can be done in several ways:

- using wipe-off pens on an overhead transparency;

- placing a blank transparency on top of a printed overhead transparency;

- using marker pens on a text written on chart paper. This provides a permanent record of the model and can be displayed for reference.

Models made in this way can be used as temporary prompts for students to refer to in their own reading, and so they facilitate the gradual transfer of responsibility from the teacher to the student.

Students can model too

Over time, and with careful continuing support, students can take over the role of modeling to make their thinking processes clear. As they develop confidence, some will internalize the modeling, while others may need verbal or written prompts. Students often find this kind of thinking easier to do than to explain. Teachers need to look for evidence that students are thinking metacognitively.

Teaching students to model

Kelvin taught his students to use key phrases as a way of making their metacognitive thinking explicit. After modeling how to do this himself and explaining why it was useful, he was able to gradually hand over the responsibility. He did this by giving specific feedback when students used these phrases independently. With prompts like "when you respond to each other in this way, you encourage the person to share their thinking, and you let them know you've been really listening," he saw the social language of the classroom change dramatically. Ultimately, they were able to use these and other phrases automatically:

- *When I read this, I wondered …*
- *I'm not sure what's happening here. I need to go back and reread that sentence.*
- *I already knew … and that helped me to understand …*
- *I'm picturing … as I read this.*

Allowing students to see how this metacognitive process works and to try it out for themselves in the relative safety of shared reading provides students with useful models that they can use and practice in their own reading.

Villaume and Brabman (2002) stress that although "modeling is one of the most explicit ways to teach a comprehension strategy", it is not enough in itself. "[C]larity emerges from teachers' abilities to facilitate conversations that reveal and extend students' understandings and that identify and address their misunderstandings" (page 674). The next chapter describes ways in which teachers can facilitate such conversations.

CHAPTER 7

Promoting Discussion with Questions and Feedback

Learning through discussion

The importance of social interaction to learning has already been mentioned. A key feature of shared reading is discussion, where the participants share and consider ideas, build on each other's contributions, and try out new ways of thinking. One of the most important reasons for using shared reading beyond the first few years of school is to improve the quality and depth of students' thinking through discussions about texts. Discussions can be initiated and kept alive in different ways. Purposeful questioning, explicit modeling, the use of encouraging prompts, and meaningful feedback are the key ways in which a teacher can engage students in conversations that will improve their thinking processes. As a result of such discussion, students develop their own questioning strategies and become more purposeful, strategic, and critical readers. This chapter examines the use of questioning and feedback in shared reading.

And the question is …

> *"Isidor Rabi, a Nobel prize-winning physicist, tells a story of when he was growing up in the Jewish ghetto of New York. When the children came home from school, their mothers would ask them, 'What did you learn in school today?' But Isidor's mother would ask him, 'What good questions did you ask today?' Dr. Rabi suggests he became a physicist and won the Nobel Prize because he was valued more for the questions he was asking than the answers he was giving."*
>
> Barell, 1988, quoted in Barbara J. Millis and Philip G. Cottell, Jr. (eds.), 1998, page 139

Questioning is probably the most common way that people learn. It develops from an early age as a key strategy in naming and understanding the world as expressed in the very young child's persistent "Why?" With the transition to school, the need to produce factual answers to teachers' questions often overrides this natural urge.

Traditionally, teachers have directed questions to students as the primary activity after reading. The kinds of questions posed often require simple recall of facts or details. Dolores Durkin's now classic research into comprehension instruction in the late 1970s revealed both the widespread practice of questioning as a test of understanding and the superficial nature of such questioning. Unfortunately, this form of questioning is still common practice in many classrooms.

The most effective questions ask students to utilize their own knowledge and ideas to address the teaching objective. Teachers who use questions strategically promote new kinds of thinking in their students and motivate their engagement in thought-provoking discussions.

Compare these examples of teacher questioning to promote discussion:

Example 1

Teacher 1: We've been learning about the Arctic for several weeks now. So is the Arctic a place where people could live easily?

Student: No.

Teacher 1: Right. What animals live in the Arctic?

Students: Wolves, polar bears …

Teacher 1: And what else? Can you find the names of some other animals that are found in the Arctic?

Example 2

Teacher 2: Let's talk about cause and effect in the Arctic. What is cause?

Student: What happens and what makes it happen?

Student: Yeah, like the reason for something, what makes it happen.

Teacher 2: Can you give me some examples from this text? What are some of the things that happen in the Arctic?

Student: It's dark all day for most of the year.

Student: And it's light all night sometimes.

Teacher 2: Right. Now, are the lengths of the days a cause of something or an effect? What are some questions you can ask yourself about that fact?

Student: Why are the nights so long? What causes it?

In the first example, the teacher's closed questions produced factual responses that relied on the students recalling and locating facts from the text. Their answers were either right or wrong, and the resulting exchange could not really be called a discussion. Although this technique is useful to review previous

learning, it does not promote independent thinking. The second example shows
questions that require thinking as well as recall. They enable students to engage
with the text, the teacher, and each other as they reevaluate their thinking to
make meaning of the text.

By the teacher's promotion of discussion and dialogue, the students begin to see
and hear various methods of understanding and connecting to the text in deeper
ways. When the teacher uses standard forms of open-ended questions, the
students can see that similar questions can be used in many different kinds of
text. Increasingly, even standardized reading tests do not simply ask students to
recall facts from the text. Many of them require students to draw conclusions, to
infer, to make connections and comparisons, and to summarize and evaluate.

Sample standardized test questions

This story contains some statements that are facts and some that are opinions.

Which statement below is an opinion?

A. The hoof prints would be half circles, split in the middle.

B. The flock had to be somewhere nearby.

C. She chewed on beef jerky.

D. They trotted along, glancing at the scenery.

Compared to coastal areas, interior areas of a large continent tend to have:

A. higher amounts of rainfall throughout the year

B. a greater incidence of fog during summer months

C. an increased risk of hurricanes during the spring months

D. more extreme temperature differences between winter and summer

---

Questions in a shared reading approach

The teacher's use of rich, open-ended questioning is a powerful technique for
engaging students in the exploration of texts in a shared reading lesson.
Although asking open-ended questions may seem a simple task, many teachers
revert to the less useful closed questions because they are what teachers are used
to using or what has been modeled for them. Framing open-ended questions
requires practice and should be an important part of the planning for a shared
reading lesson. Closed questions usually have a specific answer, whereas open-
ended questions can take the discussion to places even the teacher can't
anticipate. Questions that promote thinking and stimulate discussion should be
intentionally planned when preparing for a lesson.

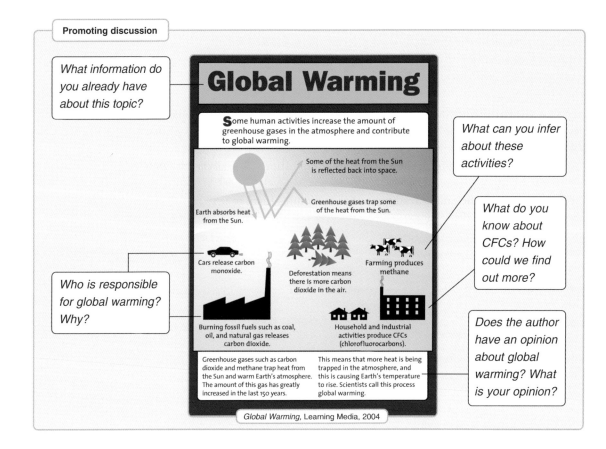

Promoting discussion

What information do you already have about this topic?

Global Warming

Some human activities increase the amount of greenhouse gases in the atmosphere and contribute to global warming.

Some of the heat from the Sun is reflected back into space.

Greenhouse gases trap some of the heat from the Sun.

Earth absorbs heat from the Sun.

Cars release carbon monoxide.

Deforestation means there is more carbon dioxide in the air.

Farming produces methane

Burning fossil fuels such as coal, oil, and natural gas releases carbon dioxide.

Household and industrial activities produce CFCs (chlorofluorocarbons).

Greenhouse gases such as carbon dioxide and methane trap heat from the Sun and warm Earth's atmosphere. The amount of this gas has greatly increased in the last 150 years.

This means that more heat is being trapped in the atmosphere, and this is causing Earth's temperature to rise. Scientists call this process global warming.

Global Warming, Learning Media, 2004

What can you infer about these activities?

What do you know about CFCs? How could we find out more?

Who is responsible for global warming? Why?

Does the author have an opinion about global warming? What is your opinion?

The impact of questions

When teachers use a variety of good questioning and prompting techniques, they can lead their students to be genuinely curious about a text. Students exposed to questioning techniques that deepen their reading experiences are more able to generate the "high quality talk" (Duke and Pearson, 2002) essential for real comprehension.

The types of questions that teachers ask students about texts have a significant impact on the students' understanding and recall of those texts. If discussion about a text is limited to questions requiring factual answers, the students tend to focus on factual details when they read. Alternatively, if the teacher uses the kind of questioning that requires a degree of inference and reflection, their students are more likely to use these behaviors in their independent reading (Duke and Pearson, 2002). Teaching students how to ask and respond to good questions can give them an internalized framework for thinking that they can use in other reading situations. Furthermore, it invites the students to become the makers of questions instead of just passive recipients. Shared reading is an approach that provides an ideal context to teach good questioning.

This internalized framework is part of what has been described earlier (see page 11) as metacognition: "[T]he metacognitive processes and strategies [are those] that allow readers to examine their understanding and adjust their approach" (International Association for the Evaluation of Educational Achievement, 2000, page 26). Metacognition does not involve students asking themselves lists of recall questions at the end of reading; rather, it requires them to ask questions before, during, and after reading. Active questioning (of the text, the author, themselves, and their peers) during the reading process needs to be modeled, practiced, and stressed with all students. For many adult readers, this is central to the enjoyment of reading. "Why did the author decide to do this?" "I wonder what this character will do next?" "How does this compare with what I already know?" Teachers can show and model the internal dialogue that happens when good readers read and make meaning of texts. This internal dialogue is what keeps readers engaged and interested in a piece of text. Good instruction on questioning during shared reading leads the students to generate their own questions. The teacher gradually steps back from directing and asking the questions and shifts the responsibility to their students.

Using questioning effectively

To work well, the process of posing and generating good questions must be planned and deliberate but also be flexible enough to respond to the students' interactions and thoughts. The number of questions should be limited to those that are most likely to foster thinking. Just because particular questions are on the planning sheet does not mean that all of them need to be asked or answered. The flow of the discussion and the way in which it supports the objective are the guiding factors. This flexibility allows for the students' questions to emerge and shape the discussion.

The following suggestions can assist the planning and use of questioning within shared reading.

- Plan the questions ahead of time. Questions should be based on the objective or purpose of the lesson. Ideas for sample questions can be recorded on a lesson plan or on a copy of the text.

- Use questions that seek descriptive, analytical, and more open answers rather than simple recall and location of facts.

- Respond positively to questions generated by the students. However, where necessary, encourage their attention away from surface level questions toward those that lead to deeper understanding or that require the student to delve deeper into a text or topic. Ask questions that seek clarification from the students, reinforcing the importance of justifying and being accountable for their ideas.

- Build on responses as opportunities arise. This could include asking students to expand on their thinking, asking them how they got to their idea, or asking further questions about their response.

Building on responses

Sandi, a grade 6 teacher, is discussing the poem *City Song* with her class.

Sandi: *I want you to give me evidence from the poem that tells us how the poet feels about the city. Tom?*

Tom: *I think she's got mixed feelings because the first stanza is kind of like a good one – a good thing about the city, then the second one's not so good, then the third one's kind of a good one, then the other one's a kind of bad one, then the last one's good, so it chops and changes.*

Sandi: *So you think there's a bit of a mix – she says some really great things about the city and also some not-so-good things? (Tom nods.) Tom, just tell me a little bit more. Why do you think this one (points to stanza two) is not such a positive verse about the city?*

Tom: *Because there's words like "litter" and "traffic," which causes pollution and stuff.*

Sandi: *So when the poet says "The hum of the traffic" – do you think that line in the poem suggests she doesn't like it, or is it just a fact about the city?*

Tom: *It could mean that she likes it and dislikes it at the same time.*

Sandi: *You're right, it could mean that. Thank you.*

- By modeling questions and feedback that go beyond mere recall, encourage the students to ask questions of each other that require higher level thinking.

Prompting student-to-student discussion

Teacher: *When I read this story, I wondered what life would have been like for the children of the early settlers. How would they cope with those long journeys in wagons? What did they do all day? I'd like you to have a brief discussion with two people near you and come up with some good questions to ask about this story. Think about the kinds of questions that really make us think and that lead us into finding out more – not the ones we can answer quickly from the text.*

The students discuss in small groups.

Stevie: *How about asking why there weren't so many children? I mean, in the pictures there are only a few kids, but there's lots of adults.*

Jackson: *Yeah, you're right – that's weird! And I'd like to ask about the wagons – how did they make them when they didn't have factories and things? Where did they get the stuff they needed to make them?*

- Teach and encourage the development of listening skills. Model what active listening looks and sounds like. Another approach is the fishbowl, which requires half the students to act as observers while the rest engage in discussion. The observers can provide constructive feedback at the end of the discussion and then switch roles with the other students for the next lesson.

- Show, through examples, that good questions are often those that lead to the places where other questions are lurking.

Questions leading to further questioning

Emma and her class were discussing the following sentence in a shared reading session: "Abandoned and mistreated pets are looked after by the animal shelter." The students had a lot of background knowledge about this topic and enthusiastically generated a variety of questions. Emma decided to use their enthusiasm to show how sharing questions in a group can inspire new thinking and deeper questioning.

Emma: *Many of your questions involve the ways shelters care for abandoned animals. While you were talking, I immediately started to wonder something else … Why would people abandon or mistreat animals in the first place? This is an example of how your questions inspired new and deeper thinking in me. Let's see if we can ask some really juicy questions of the group that will motivate even bigger and better questions in others!*

Ali: *I heard about a woman who had her pets taken away because she had so many she couldn't feed them all. If she had so many pets, doesn't that mean that she loves animals? Why would she want them to go hungry?*

Keith: *Well, maybe she lost her job and couldn't afford the food anymore …*

Emma: *I know it's tempting to try and answer each other's questions, but sometimes it's better to put the answers aside for a while and focus on how one question can lead to another. Some questions are so good and so deep that we want to savor the wondering they create. Did anyone think of a question as a result of the last question, "Why would she want them to go hungry?"*

Walter: *I wondered, "Are people so lonely that they will keep pets even if they can't care for them?"*

Emma: *Wow, now that really gets me wondering about all the reasons people mistreat animals.*

Keith: *I can't imagine hurting an animal, so I started to ask myself, "What are some of the ways to mistreat animals?"*

- Allow generous "wait time" after posing questions or asking students to generate questions. This may also include providing opportunities for students to discuss their responses in pairs or groups before sharing with the larger group. Increased wait time often results in:

- longer, more thoughtful answers being volunteered;
- more volunteers;
- responses involving higher levels of thinking;
- more student-generated questions;
- encouragement for shy or reluctant students.

- Know when to move on. Questioning the text should never be allowed to interrupt the flow of a text to such an extent that meaning and engagement are lost.

- Distribute your questions across the group but not at random. Teachers who know their students well can vary the level and complexity of questions or prompts according to the abilities of individual students.

- Don't be afraid of coming back to the same student with a follow-up question. Sometimes an extended exchange between the teacher and a single student or between two students can develop an interesting line of thinking. The rest of the group benefits from the exchange, particularly when they are expected to comment or reflect on it.

Developing a question file

Over time, teachers and their students may find it useful to accumulate a list or file of standard forms of questions to prompt discussion in shared reading. They may start out as a written list on a whiteboard or chart but, as the habit of questioning develops, it is important that students develop and internalize their own mental file that can provide thinking prompts for different purposes. This in turn helps them to develop the metacognitive skills that they can draw on whenever a text puzzles them or when they need to dig deeper to search for layers of meaning. A question file needs to be managed carefully to prevent it from becoming a checklist.

The following examples of standard questions are open rather than text specific. Therefore, teachers and students could use them with a variety of texts – fiction or nonfiction – and for various purposes. Teachers should customize this list to meet the needs of their students. They can simplify the list for less confident readers and ask more complicated or sophisticated questions of confident readers. Giving each student a bookmark with question prompts is a great way to adjust the level of questions to different reading groups.

Explaining

Why does …?

How does …?

How do you know that is true?

What evidence do you have?

Why did this happen?

Why do you think that?

What caused this?

What might be the result? Why do you think so?

Can you explain?

Generalizing

What is true about all of these?

What does that tell us about …?

What conclusions can you draw?

Classifying

Which of these go together?

How is that similar to …?

What criteria have been used to classify these?

What are the characteristics of the things in this group?

What is another example of this?

Clarifying

Why am I confused?

What made me think that?

What did the author mean by that?

Where would I go for more information?

Describing

What is … like?

What can you see?

What did you notice about …?

How would you describe …?

Inferring

Can you explain from this how …?

What do you think might be happening here?

What do you think might cause this?

How do you imagine they are feeling?

Predicting and hypothesizing

What are we going to see?

What might happen if …?

What would it be like if …?

What do you think will happen next?

Personal response

What would I do in this situation?

What are my beliefs on this topic?

How would I feel if …?

What would I be hoping for?

Could this happen to me?

Analyzing

How does the text layout help the reader?

How does the title connect with the story?

What catches my eye first? Why?

Evaluating

What were the reasons for this?

How could this be improved?

How could you justify this?

Is this the best way to …?

What did the author want me to understand? … remember? … learn?

What is the most important message in this piece?

It is important to accommodate the students' individual learning styles by giving them not only different kinds of questions but different ways to respond to questions. Some questions should ask students to pay attention to what they observe, and others should invite students to share what they feel. Certain questions can ask students to synthesize information from the text, but the teacher could connect these questions with prompts to make a judgment about the piece. For example, after reading an editorial together, the teacher could ask evaluative or personal response questions such as "Who is the intended audience for this piece?" or "What could you add to the author's argument that would be convincing to someone your age?"

Providing a variety of response options for students encourages everyone to participate in the discussion and engage personally with the text. A few simple ways in which teachers can vary the response choices include asking students to:

- think/pair/share;

- whisper to their neighbor;

- give a thumbs up if they agree – thumbs down if they don't;

- "Get your question or answer in your head. Now what's the best way to say it?";

- write in reader response logs;

- sketch what they are thinking;

- put their "heads together" to discuss for two minutes after every ten minutes of teacher modeling or class discussion. This strategy, developed especially for English language learners, gives students a chance to process new information (Bechtel, 2000). Encourage students to discuss in their primary language if they have a same-language peer in the class.

Making discussion work for everyone

Many students, particularly in upper elementary grades, have never learned how to engage with texts in any depth. The reasons for difficulties in this area are often complex. For example, the demand for recall may have challenged or bored some students so much that they gave up expecting to find meaning or value in reading long ago. This phenomenon can be particularly true for struggling or reluctant readers. Alternatively, such difficulties may have arisen from issues of language or culture not taken into account in the instruction.

Another reason for the lack of engagement may be the nature of the reading tasks presented to students whose mastery of English is not yet complete. Often, English language learners are given reading tasks that do not have scope for rich discussion. Instruction that focuses on surface features (for example, correct pronunciation) does not provide opportunity for the expression and exchange of ideas that leads to higher order thinking.

It is critical that the kinds of questions teachers ask and the feedback they provide are appropriate to the needs, cultures, and experiences of the students. Teachers' questions and feedback must lead students to learn how to make meaning and find value in reading for themselves. The support (from the teacher and from peers) available in shared reading makes it a good choice of instructional strategy. By using appropriate texts and carefully planned discussions, a teacher can take the needs of a wide variety of learners into account in a shared reading lesson.

Encouraging meaningful participation

Methods for encouraging meaningful participation from English language learners include:

- Providing significant wait time after a prompt or question.
- Allowing students a chance to formulate and then practice their comments in pairs before sharing them with the whole group.
- Encouraging students to think in their first language and share their response with a same-language peer.
- Asking questions that deliberately draw upon the cultural and personal experiences of students.
- Limiting the times when the English language learner's speech is corrected. (Make the focus on content and ideas, not presentation.)
- Encouraging and rewarding risk taking in classroom discussions.
- Using scaffolds, such as graphic organizers, to demonstrate how thoughts can be planned and structured for clarity. (Make these available for students to use during discussions.)

Feedback

Good questioning is only part of the mix that makes for a compelling shared reading discussion. In response to questions, participants may offer responses that explain, predict, suggest, clarify, and much more. What happens next is just as important as the nature of the questioning. The ways that the teacher responds to student contributions are another factor in directing and enhancing the learning within a shared reading lesson. Giving good feedback is more than simply responding to students' answers or to their contributions to a discussion. It means affirming their attempts at using new thinking and new strategies, modeling for them how readers and writers think, guiding them to find other ways of looking at the issue, and inviting them to direct their own future learning. Effective feedback is a very powerful tool for motivating students and advancing their learning.

The primary purpose of feedback is not to indicate whether learners are right or wrong but to enable them to reflect on their use of strategies for reading and writing and on their learning. Feedback involves conveying information to learners about where and when to use their knowledge and strategies. Effective feedback can provide a model of how good readers and writers think.

Ministry of Education, 2003, page 84

The feedback provided in shared reading is a form of scaffolding and therefore needs to relate to the lesson's purpose. Feedback should aim to increase the students' control of their own learning. Simply praising a contribution is not going to let the students know any more about themselves as learners although it may (for a short time only) improve their self-esteem. On the other hand, effective feedback gives honest, constructive information about performance, which is a far more useful form of encouragement. Specific feedback should build the students' awareness of *why* their contributions were effective. Making the value of their contribution explicit opens the way for students to become metacognitive, that is, to be aware of and regulate their own thinking and learning. It also builds self-esteem.

Using explicit feedback

That's an interesting comment – it makes me wonder what you were thinking as you read this passage. Can you tell us more?

I like the connections you made with the story we read last week. You've shown us how it helps us to understand this story better: thank you!

Right! You're thinking about what you're doing when you read a complex sentence so you can make sense of it as you read.

OK, so when you say "the scientists couldn't understand why it was happening," can you explain that a bit more? What words in the text made you think they didn't understand?

By using and explicitly teaching students about feedback, the teacher can encourage them to give good feedback to each other. At first it may be necessary to model phrases and provide the students with the language of effective feedback.

The language of effective feedback

I like the way …

I hadn't thought of it that way …

What if you tried …?

It would have been even better if …

With time, the use of these scaffolds can be reduced so that the students learn to create authentic and appropriate feedback independently.

One of the most effective outcomes of specific and thoughtful feedback is that it motivates students to learn more. A standard compliment like "good work" may, in fact, encourage the student to stay stuck where they are, employing the same vocabulary, response, or strategies over and over. Feedback that directs the students to reflect on their learning can inspire them to ask: "What strategy did I use that helped? What can I do to learn more? How can I be even more successful?"

Prompting reflection

Prompts that can lead to the type of reflection outlined above might sound like:

I hadn't thought of it from that perspective. You just helped me add to my thinking!

Where did you get that idea? What made you think that?

Tell us more about that …

I liked the way you tried something new. What else could you try to help you figure out that word?

Can you describe that in more detail?

How does your response relate to our purpose today?

A good rule of thumb for teachers practicing effective feedback is to make sure that their comments always:

- help the students become more aware of their own learning;
- refer the students back to the lesson's objective.

CHAPTER 8

Competencies for Comprehension

Characteristics of effective readers

Effective readers have developed the following competencies that help them to make meaning:

- Reading fluently. This includes decoding words rapidly and accurately and recognizing increasingly large numbers of words on sight. Without this ability, reading is either not happening or happens at such a slow, letter-by-letter rate that the learner is unable to make meaning as she or he reads. Fluency also refers to the flow of the reading. Readers who are competent decoders and have good comprehension read with a smooth flow, using expression and intonation appropriately. Shared reading is often used in the early years to build fluency in decoding, and it can be used at all levels to model smooth, expressive, accurate reading.

- Drawing upon a wide vocabulary base. Although research shows that people learn much of their vocabulary incidentally, it also shows that those with a wide vocabulary are better readers than those whose vocabulary is limited. (For example, see Graves and Watts-Taffe, 2002.) Deliberate teaching of vocabulary has been shown to increase comprehension (Pressley, 2002). The role that shared reading can play in vocabulary instruction is discussed later in this chapter.

- Relating their knowledge about the world to their reading. Knowing about the world (and the ability to make connections to it) affects the ability of learners to understand what they read. Moustafa (1997) cites several experiments carried out in the 1970s, which showed that children with prior knowledge of a topic were better able to answer questions after reading a passage on the topic than those without such knowledge. Ways that existing knowledge can be brought to mind, strengthened, and developed through shared reading are discussed later in this chapter.

- Applying a variety of comprehension strategies. Mastering these strategies and being able to use them in integrated, coordinated ways is essential to comprehension. Comprehension strategies and the ways that they can be taught and supported by shared reading are discussed in chapter 9.

- Monitoring and mending when meaning is lost. This is something that good readers do automatically. Students who have experienced reading as a chore to be endured – one that requires them only to find answers to superficial questions – are probably not aware of the depth of meaning that can be gained by reading. They may not even expect to find meaning in print. Monitoring for meaning, rereading to work out unfamiliar words or language structures, and asking for clarification are all reading strategies that can be taught using a shared reading approach.

- Navigating a variety of texts for diverse purposes. Exposure to a diversity of texts helps build vocabulary, knowledge of the world, and familiarity with the ways that texts work. Shared reading allows a teacher to use a wide variety of texts and purposes to ensure that students have this exposure. Texts selected need to be worthwhile and well suited to the purpose of the lesson.

- Integrating print and non-print information. As nonfiction texts become more complex, the information contained in visuals needs to be understood and integrated into the overall sense of the text. By modeling how to do this in shared reading, teachers can give students opportunities to learn and practice ways of integrating multiple forms of information themselves.

In the remainder of this chapter, two of these competencies are examined as examples of how shared reading can be used to support comprehension. These competencies are the building of vocabulary (working out words together) and the use of prior knowledge.

Working out words together

A number of studies have documented the links between poor vocabulary knowledge and poor reading achievement. Graves and Watts-Taffe conclude that "the task of learning vocabulary is huge … students learn approximately 3,000 to 4,000 words each year, accumulating a reading vocabulary of approximately 25,000 words by the end of elementary school and approximately 50,000 words by the end of high school" (Graves and Watts-Taffe, 2002, page 142).

Students work out the meanings of many unfamiliar words when they are simply reading or being read to. This happens spontaneously. These modest gains in vocabulary knowledge occur without explicit instruction (Swanborn and de Glopper, 1999). However, when a teacher gives some instruction, the rate jumps dramatically – Elley's 1989 research showed that the vocabulary acquisition rate increased by 40 percent when teachers explained the vocabulary as they read stories aloud. For students from diverse language backgrounds, and for others struggling with fluency, comprehension, and writing in particular, instruction that extends vocabulary and language knowledge is especially important and worthwhile. The words selected for instruction must have some meaning for the students, and the instruction should be reinforced by being used elsewhere.

There are many ways in which teachers can use shared reading to increase vocabulary and extend knowledge about how language works. Some of these are outlined below.

Modeling oral reading

The teacher can model good oral reading and allow the students to follow with their eyes to teach them how to pronounce unfamiliar words. Often simply hearing an unfamiliar word read aloud while seeing it in print provides a point of reference when the students come across the same word in another context.

Explaining unfamiliar words

The teacher can pause to explain unfamiliar words while reading.

Unfamiliar words

Words to explain in this example could include:

- sextant (using the explanation in the text as a guide)
- seventeenth century
- angle
- navigation tables
- position.

Sailors have been using sextants since the seventeenth century to help them find their way. A sextant measures the angle of the sun, the moon, or certain stars. If you also know the date and the time, it is possible to use math and a set of navigation tables to work out your exact position.

from *Finding Your Way* by John Bonallack, 2000

Within a short piece of text, however, it's not advisable to explain every unfamiliar word unless the purpose of the lesson is to identify and explain specialized vocabulary. In fact, meaning can be gained without the reader knowing every word. Words that are important to the meaning of the text, that are the topic of study, or that are out of the realm of the students' experiences could be explained if context clues are not helpful. If a piece has too many unknown words, it may be too difficult to use with this group of students.

Highlighting unfamiliar words

The teacher can highlight unfamiliar words to teach the students how to work out the word meanings from the context. Many multisyllabic words can be worked out by highlighting root words, prefixes and suffixes, or by exploring derivations. Showing students that they can work out meaning in these ways is a good strategy because it can easily be transferred to their own reading. Highlight potentially difficult words before starting the shared reading lesson. After reading, return to the highlighted word and, with the students, use the context, etymology, or syntax to find its meaning.

Working out words

"Instablility is bad for kids; changing schools is a form of instability …"

In an article from *Time for Kids* that Jeannie wanted to share with her fifth grade class, the word "instability" appeared in relation to students who change schools a lot. Although many of her students could make connections with the topic, she guessed that this word would stump quite a few. Jeannie highlighted the word on the overhead transparency and paused when she came to it half way through reading the article.

I know many of you won't know what this word means in this context, but I'm going to ask you to pass over it until we come to the end of the article.

Later, she returned to the word as promised, but she approached it indirectly in order to build connections with the concept.

Now, we've heard of things and maybe even people described as "unstable." Can you think of any examples?

Right, a building can be unstable. An area where there are lots of earthquakes can be unstable. Yes, sometimes we talk about people who are unstable. Can you guess what "unstable" might mean?

Good, I like the way you broke the word into parts to help you figure out the meaning. The prefix "un" usually means not. So something that is unstable is not stable, not dependable.

Now let's go back to the word from the text: "instability." Given what you know about the meaning of unstable, think about the topic of this article. How are the two ideas related?

Exactly! Coming from a "stable home" is very important for kids. Being able to depend on your family and count on your life staying the same are factors that make for a stable environment. So what would an "unstable environment" be like?

Yes, nice job making a connection between our discussion and the text. An unstable environment might mean changing school a lot. So what do you think "instability" means, then? Why would it be bad for kids?

from *Time for Kids*, September 19, 2003, Volume 9, Number 2

Teaching specialized vocabulary

Vocabulary that is specific to a text or a topic can be taught explicitly. Subject teachers can use this strategy to ensure that their students understand any specialized vocabulary before they are asked to read and use information. Shared reading is an effective way to teach specialized vocabulary because the teacher can provide a definition or explanation as well as a context that helps the students understand the words and their applications. This vocabulary work can be done as a separate word study, but if it is linked to the shared reading of a text containing specialist vocabulary, the teaching is reinforced. Listing topic-specific vocabulary on wall charts is an effective follow-up and provides a ready reference when the students need to use the words in their own writing. Ensure that the students have opportunities to reinforce and use these words in further learning situations.

> Much of the clay we use for pottery comes from granite – one of the hardest rocks in the world. Granite formed millions of years ago, when very hot, molten minerals were trapped deep within the Earth's rocky crust. As the molten rock slowly cooled, minerals such as quartz and feldspar formed into the crystalline rock we call granite.
>
> from *From Rock to Rock* by Jane Thompson, 2000

The text about volcano formation from which this extract is taken could be used in shared reading to identify and discuss new vocabulary. New words could be recorded as they are encountered and definitions of the words displayed alongside. Teaching students to skim the text for unknown vocabulary words can alert them to use their prior knowledge, use the index or glossary, or to seek other help to make meaning of the text.

Using word play

Word play, such as jokes and puns, can be used as a focus of several shared reading lessons. This is an effective way to foster "word consciousness" (Graves and Watts-Taffe, 2002) which, among other things, involves becoming metacognitive about the use of words and their meanings. By using shared reading, a teacher can introduce the whole class to a study and then provide opportunities for individuals or small groups to develop ideas further.

Working out words

An easy way to have fun with words is to use puns. Today we're going to look at how an author uses puns to create humor. A pun is a joke made by using the different meanings for the same word (or words that sound the same but have different meanings). For example: "How do you stop a rhino from charging? Take away its credit card." There are two meanings to the word charging. That's what makes the joke work. Let's look at this ad and see if we can identify the puns.

Rovermatic
Dog-ate-my-homework Kit

Does this sound like you?

You live in an apartment, so the fiercest pet you own is a goldfish. You've got to leave for school in five minutes, and you haven't done your homework? Hot diggity dog – have we got just the thing for you. Take the "work" out of homework – try the Rovermatic Dog-ate-my-homework Kit.

Each kit comes with:

Pooch pawprint stamp – with mud-colored ink that won't stain your clothes

The Lassie-rator real-looking champ marks

Doggie drool – a big bottle of slobber that will smudge any writing

Buy now, and you'll never be hounded by homework again.
Only $19.95

from *Kids Inc.* by Ross Bennett, Maryanne Rossiter, and Micaela Young, 2001

To lacerate something means to cut it. How does the ad use this word to make a pun?

I'll give you a hint to start. Rover is a commonly used name for a dog. Try to find the pun that uses Rover while we read the ad together.

Being "hounded" means to be bothered or nagged by someone. Why is this sentence a pun?

94

Prior knowledge: the more you know, the more you learn

> We'd just start jamming, then put it all down on an old eight track. Then we'd go back and find the parts we liked and load all that into samplers, and that was how we'd make the tracks. That worked for six of the eight tracks – the other two were started on sequencers and finished that way too. Ken pillaged his back catalogue for the right hook, and I took snippets from other masters, and the more we tried the more it worked.

This extract was taken from an unpublished interview in which two rock musicians spoke about how they made their latest CD. For a reader with some knowledge of rock music, it's probably easy to understand. For anyone without that specialist knowledge, it may be partly incomprehensible, although knowing words such as samplers, sequence, pillage, and snippets from other contexts may help with working out meaning in this text.

What students bring to their reading has an enormous influence on how much they understand when they read. When teachers wish to introduce topics or concepts about which their students have little or no prior knowledge or direct experience, they need to build bridges to help their students move from what they know to what they don't know. In other words, teachers need to use the familiar to help students discover and understand the unknown.

Accessing what the students know already

Sometimes known as "activating prior knowledge" or "making connections with the text," the purpose of many shared reading lessons is to help make connections so that students can find a way in to texts they would otherwise struggle to comprehend. Students often have knowledge about a topic that can be explored and developed to reveal connections with a new text. The use of these connections needs to be valued and reinforced because students can all too frequently be satisfied with a superficial level of comprehension, not realizing (or caring) that there are deeper levels to be explored.

In the example below, Kathleen knew that most of her students would have no experience of truly freezing weather conditions. Most had grown up on the California-Mexico border where the weather is mild all year round. She had to teach a unit about Antarctica as part of the school's social studies curriculum, so she spent time carefully working with her class to help them identify words and ideas in the text that they could relate to. Note that she explained why she was doing this first.

Making connections

Kathleen: As you know, we've been looking at books about Antarctica for our new social studies unit. Some of this stuff you won't be familiar with at all, but I want to show you how you can use what you know to get a handle on it. I've made overheads of some sections in the book I read aloud yesterday so that we can look at them more closely. Let's read the section on temperature together first.

(Kathleen reads the page off the overhead.)

What were some of the things you got from this, using what you know?

Jose: It's below zero. In summer, the temperature doesn't go much above freezing.

Maria: If you take hot water outside, it would freeze.

Kathleen: What would that be like?

The students discussed their own experiences of extreme cold, mostly related to a domestic freezer. Then Kathleen read the page again, pausing to check for understanding.

Kathleen: "... metal sticks to bare flesh." What does this mean?

Jose: It would stick to skin.

Kathleen: What's this word "bare" mean?

Jose: Skin that hasn't got anything on it – no clothes.

Carmel: Like sometimes when I go for ice or something in the freezer, my fingers stick to it? But they're not metal ...

Kathleen: That's great! You know what it would feel like to have something real cold stick to your skin. I bet you've all had that experience, right? That's information you bring to this topic.

Kathleen: "... fillings can fall out of teeth." What do you think fillings might be?

Carlos: Little metal things.

Kathleen: How many of you knew that word? Why would they fall out?

96

Building new knowledge

The most obvious way to build knowledge is to provide direct experiences – a visit to a theme park, organizing a party, a hike in the woods. This is not always possible. Next best is to provide opportunities for learning through books, television programs, videos, illustrated talks by people who have particular experiences, music, and other more accessible activities for the classroom.

Instruction in using what students know

This is different from the first two suggestions in that it involves explicitly teaching the use of prior knowledge as a comprehension strategy. Students do not always realize that it's important to connect new material with what they already know, particularly if the material originates from different curriculum areas. The active recalling of what they know, or the conscious connecting of new knowledge with old, can help students make sense of and remember what they read. It's not that they don't have relevant knowledge; it simply doesn't occur to them that using what they know will help them to learn. If teachers model their use of what they already know as they approach a new text, students learn to value and bring forward their own connections. Shared reading can allow a teacher to model and demonstrate this important comprehension strategy.

Using what you know

Sometimes when you're trying to understand a passage more deeply, you can be helped by background knowledge that you hadn't even thought about using. For example, when reading this book about the Statue of Liberty, I wondered what could help me understand why she was such an important symbol for immigrants. I've never visited Ellis Island or the Statue. Furthermore, I don't know anyone who was an immigrant.

In fact, I have lots of background knowledge that can help me. I just need to remember to use it! I recently finished reading a book by Patricia Reilly Giff called Nory Ryan's Song *about an Irish girl and her family suffering through the potato famine in Ireland. Their life was unimaginably hard. They had no food, no money, and no hope for a better future in Ireland. Nory was desperate to escape and join her eldest sister in America. I'm now imagining how beautiful and inspiring the Statue of Liberty must have seemed to her after all the hardship she had to endure to get to America. When I think about Nory, I have a much deeper understanding of what the text means when it says, "This statue is the most amazing thing you've ever seen!"*

A Warm Welcome

Imagine that you and your family lived a hundred years ago. For weeks, you've been traveling by ship toward the United States, a country that is to become your new home. The ship is crowded, and there have been times when you've thought that your journey across the Atlantic Ocean would never end.

Then, after seeing nothing but the ocean for a very long time, your tired eyes make out a huge statue of a woman dressed in flowing robes and wearing a crown that has seven spikes. In one hand, she's holding a giant torch, and in the other, a book.

This statue is the most amazing thing you've ever seen.

For more than a hundred years, the Statue of Liberty has welcomed immigrants from all over the world to the United States.

from *The Statue of Liberty* by Rob Lang, 2002

Think about a time you heard or read a story of real hardship. Now imagine seeing a symbol of freedom and hope like the Statue of Liberty for the first time. How do you think you would feel? What would she represent for you?

98

CHAPTER 9

Teaching Comprehension Strategies

Comprehension strategies

Comprehension strategies are specific, learned procedures that foster active, competent, self-regulated, and intentional reading. Classroom teachers implement comprehension strategy instruction by demonstrating, modeling, or guiding their use during the reading of a text.

Trabasso and Bouchard, 2002, quoted in Block and Pressley, 2002, page 177

This chapter suggests a framework for teaching comprehension strategies and highlights the role of shared reading within it. The framework comes with a strong caution. Effective teaching is not a matter of applying a formula, recipe, or prescription. The framework described here is intended to show that shared reading is one of a variety of teaching strategies and approaches and is situated in a context of purposeful, meaningful, and enjoyable interactions. Rather than following rigid divisions between the elements outlined below, teachers are urged to use what they know about their students, about literacy instruction, and about the texts and purposes they have selected to make reading as interesting and effective as possible.

The framework

Explicit instruction only works when careful planning and assessment have taken place and when opportunities are given to explain, model, and practice. The framework described below uses elements described by various researchers as useful steps in the teaching of strategies. (See for example, Pearson and Gallagher 1983; Dowhower, 1999; Harvey and Goudvis, 2000; Duke and Pearson, 2002.) As Duke and Pearson emphasize, "good comprehension instruction includes both explicit instruction in specific comprehension strategies and a great deal of time and opportunity for actual reading, writing, and discussion of text" (page 207). Dowhower's 1999 paper on teaching students to be strategic reinforces that they develop a strategic approach to reading through a combination of being explicitly instructed and through being encouraged to generate their own mastery of the strategies they have been taught. The following framework[2] represents this process, and shows the place of shared reading within it.

Stages in the framework

The process of teaching and learning outlined above involves six stages:

1. **Explaining:** The teacher states the strategy to be taught and explains briefly why it is useful in the context of reading. The teacher explains how the strategy relates to their current reading needs.

2. **Modeling:** The teacher models the strategy, for example, by thinking out loud while reading. She or he makes the thinking explicit and visible.

3. **Guided practice:** The teacher provides encouragement and support as the students try using the strategy themselves.

4. **Student demonstration:** The students show how they can use the strategy individually or in groups.

5. **Independent use:** The students use the strategy without support or prompting.

6. **Integration:** The students internalize the strategy and integrate it with all the other ways they have learned to make meaning from texts.

This outline should not imply that each stage happens only once. Sometimes teachers may need to model strategies several times using different pieces of text, and some students may need more guidance than others.

In Figure 9.1, the shaded areas show where these stages in teaching and learning a new strategy can be woven into a literacy program that includes multiple opportunities for instruction and practice.

---

[2]Aspects of this model are adapted from Duke, N. K. and Pearson, P. D. (2002). *"Effective practices for developing reading comprehension."* In A. E. Farstrup and S. Jay Samuels *What Research Has to Say about Reading Instruction* (3rd edition, page 205–242). Copyright 2002 by the International Reading Association. Adapted with permission.

Figure 9.1 Strategy Instruction Framework

	EXPLAINING	MODELING	GUIDED PRACTICE	STUDENT DEMONSTRATION	INDEPENDENT USE	INTEGRATION
READ ALOUD						
SHARED READING						
GUIDED READING (WITH THE TEACHER)						
LITERACY TASKS, INCLUDING GROUP WORK						
INDEPENDENT READING						

The framework allows for teaching approaches that include:

- whole-class teaching (read aloud, shared reading, mini-lessons);

- small-group, teacher-guided instruction (guided reading, shared reading);

- small-group reciprocal teaching or cooperative learning (book clubs, paired reading, literature circles);

- independent activity or task work, such as assignments;

- completely independent reading for research, pleasure, or other purposes.

When the classroom program incorporates subjects such as math, science, and social studies there are many opportunities to reinforce new learning. The teacher can reduce the amount of support or guidance according to the difficulty of the task and the needs of the students. Teachers can use the framework in flexible ways and teach reading strategies in the context of real reading, not as ends in themselves.

The following example demonstrates the way a teacher could use a variety of texts to introduce one specific comprehension strategy (making inferences) using the framework described above.

Example: making inferences

Making inferences or "reading between the lines" is an important comprehension strategy, used by competent readers of all ages.

As students make inferences, they should be learning to create their own meanings from texts by combining what they already know with what is written in the text. To do this, readers pull together many cognitive activities such as predicting, interpreting, hypothesizing, and evaluating.

Explain the strategy

Tell the students that good readers usually read more than just the words on the page: they use what they already know as a way of gaining more meaning from the text. They "read between the lines" or fill in the gaps to work out things that the author hasn't told them, to guess what might have happened before, or to work out more about the characters. Good readers learn from what the author implies as well as from what is directly stated. Explain that this is called making inferences or inferring meaning. It is a hard concept to explain, so it's best to keep the explanation brief, then use examples to illustrate it. Explain that you have noticed that many of them are having trouble with this in their reading so this is why you have decided to work on it together.

Model its use

Using shared reading with an enlarged text that provides good examples, read the text through first so the students can gain a sense of the meaning. Reread all or parts of the text and pause to think out loud about what you could infer from the text. This can be done by asking questions of yourself or the text. Phrase your thinking aloud in ways that you want the students to use themselves. Don't pause too often or you risk losing meaning and interest. Continue to model in this way as you read a variety of texts over several days. In the examples on page 103, enlarged texts (or parts of texts) were used in shared reading.

How I Met Archie

Chapter One

Mom was glad she had a new job. I wasn't.
"You'll be fine, Alice," she said through her new lipstick.
"Mrs. Lilly is a very nice lady."
"How do you know?" I said. "She could be a monster.
She might be a crazy driver. She could be ..."
There was a knock on the door, and Mrs. Lilly came in.
Mom fussed. "Have you got your lunchbox? You'll
need your sweater."
I rolled my eyes. "Take it easy, Mom."
Mrs. Lilly smiled. I didn't smile back.
We followed Mom to the elevator. She was wearing a
skirt, and she click-clicked along in her high-heeled
shoes. She didn't look like Mom at all. In the basement,
she kissed me goodbye and walked to her car.
"Good luck at the newspaper," I said. I really hoped
she'd hate her new job.

Anna Kenna, 1999

Mom is starting a new job, and she says that Alice will be fine because Mrs. Lilly is a nice lady. I can infer that Mrs. Lilly is a new sitter. I know that parents often employ a sitter if they can't be home for their kids. I've used the words in the text and my own background knowledge and prior experience to make this inference.

I'm inferring that Alice's mother has been an at-home Mom for some time and that the new job means a big change in the family. The text is written in the first person – it's as if Alice is talking to me, the reader, so I learn a lot about her attitude. I also know how I felt when my mom went to work. From all this, I can infer that Alice doesn't want her mother to go to work and doesn't want to have a sitter.

Tasmanian Devils

The Tasmanian devil got its name because of the horrible noises it makes in the forest at night. It can look very scary when it opens its mouth, showing its sharp teeth. But Tasmanian devils are not as fierce or dangerous as they seem. They are only the size of a small dog and are mainly scavengers – they clean up the remains of animals that have been killed by other predators.

Rod Morris, 1999

From this paragraph and the photograph, I learn that Tasmanian devils are small animals that are pretty harmless to humans. I infer, though, that people are often afraid of them. There is specific information about their size and what they eat and do, and I add to that what I know about human attitudes towards animals that make scary noises and bare their teeth. I'm also thinking about the name that humans have given this animal – it supports my inference that people think the animal is fierce, dangerous, and bad.

Guided practice of the strategy

Ask the students to try using the strategy themselves with your guidance. This is best done in a shared reading lesson with the whole class or in smaller groups. Encourage the students to think out loud and to explain how they arrived at the inferences they make. This will be done initially by using the questions or phrasings that you modeled. You can use graphic organizers to guide and record this thinking.

MAKING INFERENCES

	The text says ...	I know ...	I can infer ...
How I Met Archie	• Mom is glad she has a new job, but Alice isn't. • Mrs. Lilly is a new person. • Alice thinks Mrs. Lilly will be awful.	• Parents sometimes hire sitters when they go to work. • I preferred it when my mom was at home for me.	• Mrs. Lilly is a new sitter for Alice.
	• Mom's job is new. • Mom's lipstick is new. • Mom is fussing over Alice. • Alice isn't used to mom being dressed up.	• Moms can get anxious when they leave their kids with other people.	• Mom has been an at-home mom until now. • Mom is nervous about her new job.
Tasmanian Devils	• It got its name from the horrible noise it makes. • But it's not fierce and dangerous.	• A Tasmanian devil is a cartoon character that acts crazy.	• Maybe the animal has a reputation it doesn't deserve.
	• It's the size of a small dog.	• I wouldn't be intimidated by a small dog.	• There's no reason to fear Tasmanian devils.
	• They are scavengers.	• Scavengers eat dead things.	• A Tasmanian devil is probably not going to attack a big, live human.

Student demonstration of the strategy

Shared and guided reading are the best approaches to use for this because you are able to give the students opportunities to demonstrate their own thinking and you can reinforce their use of inferences. You can also provide more or less assistance depending on individual needs.

Independent use of the strategy

Select activities – such as the examples below – that will require your students to make inferences.

- Write a persuasive paragraph encouraging people to think differently about Tasmanian devils.

- Rewrite the start of *How I Met Archie* from Mrs. Lilly's point of view.

- Use a highlighter pen and a photocopy of the text to mark up the places where you made inferences.

Comprehension strategies in context

Competent adult readers use multiple comprehension strategies in broad contexts that include their interests and needs, social interactions, motivations, and many other factors (Dowhower, 2002). Villaume and Brabham (2002) have noted the pitfalls in teaching comprehension strategies as discrete functions to be performed "in perfunctory rather than thoughtful ways" (page 672). They reflect on a need for teaching that does not simply teach strategies but "can transform students' dispositions towards reading."

Students can be taught to process text using comprehension strategies to gain and maintain meaning. However teachers need to constantly remind themselves and their students that strategies are tools and not ends in themselves. Susan Zimmermann (Keene and Zimmermann, 1997, page 216) reflects on the ways that she uses strategies as she reads: "They intertwine and merge and I switch quickly among them, frequently using them simultaneously." Keene and Zimmermann's central metaphor of a mosaic epitomizes this approach to making meaning. It is this kind of synthesis and automaticity that teachers should aim to demonstrate and foster in their teaching of comprehension strategies.

Teachers who over emphasize the use of one strategy can give their students the impression that reading is all about getting the strategy use right (pleasing the teacher) rather than getting the meaning. Individual strategies can be highlighted through use of methods described in this chapter, but instruction should continue beyond practicing single strategies to integrating many. As one literacy consultant pointed out:

Strategy teaching becomes meaningless if it results in the whole class putting little stickies through their books in places where they visualized or made an inference or a connection but with no idea why they've done this, or how the strategies can help them read better. Strategies can't be taught in isolation: when we read, we are integrating many at once. Older kids really need support to do this: this is where shared reading comes in.

Literacy consultant, New York City, 2002

The ease with which competent readers make meaning belies the fact that complex processing is occurring as they read. For example, making an inference involves several strategies working together. Questioning the text, relating what is read to what the reader already knows, making connections, and visualizing are just some of the things that may be passing through the reader's mind. Therefore teaching comprehension strategies is usually not about teaching something new. It's about teaching students how to bring together the strategies they already know in order to make meaning on a more sophisticated level.

Teachers need to provide just enough instruction to ensure that their students understand how a particular strategy can help them. They should then monitor their students' use and integration of that strategy and provide opportunities for practice in many contexts. Rather than teaching students what they already know or can do, strategic and powerful instruction comes from building on the known to support students as they continue to learn more about reading.

Careful instruction with many opportunities to practice should lead to students becoming metacognitive: thinking about how they are thinking as they read so that they can make any modifications needed along the way. Teachers can use the framework described in this chapter as a starting point as they guide their students into deeper levels of meaning and into more integrated, conscious ways of using the skills, strategies, and knowledge they already possess. Students need to be continually reminded that reading requires integrating many strategies rather than relying on one.

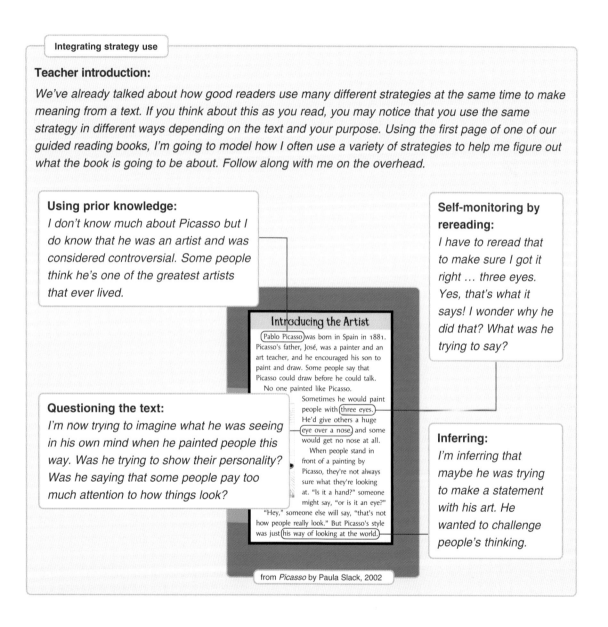

Integrating strategy use

Teacher introduction:

We've already talked about how good readers use many different strategies at the same time to make meaning from a text. If you think about this as you read, you may notice that you use the same strategy in different ways depending on the text and your purpose. Using the first page of one of our guided reading books, I'm going to model how I often use a variety of strategies to help me figure out what the book is going to be about. Follow along with me on the overhead.

Using prior knowledge:

I don't know much about Picasso but I do know that he was an artist and was considered controversial. Some people think he's one of the greatest artists that ever lived.

Self-monitoring by rereading:

I have to reread that to make sure I got it right ... three eyes. Yes, that's what it says! I wonder why he did that? What was he trying to say?

Introducing the Artist

Pablo Picasso was born in Spain in 1881. Picasso's father, José, was a painter and an art teacher, and he encouraged his son to paint and draw. Some people say that Picasso could draw before he could talk. No one painted like Picasso.

Sometimes he would paint people with three eyes. He'd give others a huge eye over a nose, and some would get no nose at all.

When people stand in front of a painting by Picasso, they're not always sure what they're looking at. "Is it a hand?" someone might say, "or is it an eye?" "Hey," someone else will say, "that's not how people really look." But Picasso's style was just his way of looking at the world.

Questioning the text:

I'm now trying to imagine what he was seeing in his own mind when he painted people this way. Was he trying to show their personality? Was he saying that some people pay too much attention to how things look?

Inferring:

I'm inferring that maybe he was trying to make a statement with his art. He wanted to challenge people's thinking.

from *Picasso* by Paula Slack, 2002

When teachers give their students opportunities and encouragement to experience the interactions and motivations that give strategy use context and meaning, they are working out meaning together. Shared reading is an approach that allows this to happen.

CHAPTER 10

Reading and Writing: Reciprocal Processes

The connections

The overriding questions that teachers want students to engage with when exploring text are "How does this writer express ideas or observations?" and "How can I use those techniques to enrich my own writing?" The teacher's job is to make the features of the text accessible to the students through engagement and deconstruction.

Jayne Jackson, deputy principal, in Ministry of Education, 2002, page 9

Reading, writing, speaking, and listening all make up separate yet equally valuable parts of a comprehensive literacy program in the classroom. Shared reading can support writing and vice versa. When students explore these connections through shared reading, the resulting discussions can inform their own writing. In particular, shared reading can help teachers improve the quality of their students' writing by demonstrating the reciprocal nature of reading and writing. Effective teachers make the connections between reading and writing explicit on a daily basis, helping their students learn how to read like writers and write like readers.

Opportunities to read and write

Teachers can use the interplay between shared reading and shared writing (where the teacher leads the class in composing a text together) to seize many serendipitous teaching moments. In the following example, the teacher used the interest and curiosity of her students to facilitate an authentic learning opportunity. In addition, the flexibility of shared reading and writing allowed her to carry this learning across the curriculum.

Learning across the curriculum

Michelle's class of ten year olds were putting on a play with their drama teacher. Several students were particularly interested in what happened behind the scenes. As a result, Michelle encouraged them to carry out research on the Internet and in the school library to find information about the use of stage makeup. They found many examples of instructions for applying theatrical makeup.

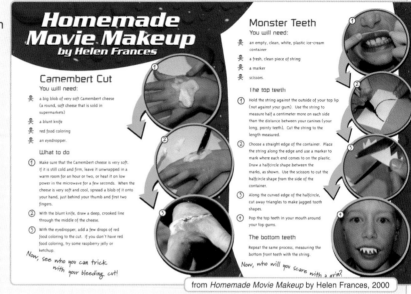

from *Homemade Movie Makeup* by Helen Frances, 2000

Michelle saw this as an ideal opportunity to teach the class about writing procedural texts (instructions). She copied one of the articles her students had found onto overhead transparencies and used it for shared reading. The purpose was to identify the features of a procedural text.

Guided by carefully focused questioning from Michelle, the students were able to examine and identify the unique features of instructions. From this discussion, they generated a list of their observations, which Michelle wrote on the whiteboard. Michelle built on what her students already knew about this text form and focused on specific language structures.

As Michelle drew attention to the text features, the students were able to see exactly why and how this form was different from other text forms. As a follow-up from the shared reading lesson, Michelle asked the students to find other examples of instructions. This yielded examples as diverse as recipes and manuals for using a video camera. The students were able to see that the examples all used a similar format. Now the students had the foundation to write their own set of instructions. Some chose to use a graphic organizer (see pages 36–37) to support their writing, but others felt confident enough to dive into their first draft using the list of features as a guide.

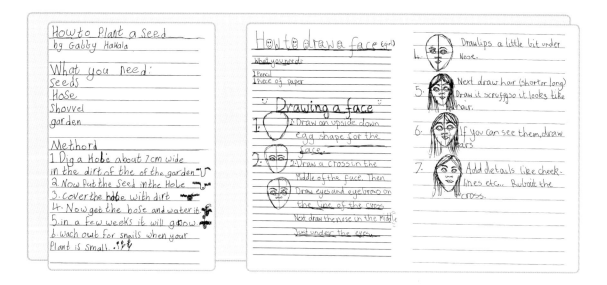

Using texts as models for writing

When as adults we are challenged to write in an unfamiliar genre or style, many
of us search for models of what others have done. We use these to help us find
appropriate style, language, tone, punctuation, and layout. Shared reading
provides an excellent opportunity to explore models of good writing in many
different genres, forms, and styles. The act of observing what writers do
enhances the interactive aspect of reading and strengthens the relationships that
exist between reading and writing. In addition, this exploratory process makes
the craft of writing more apparent to students, who may have no idea how to
improve their own writing or how reading informs writing. By studying a wide
variety of writing through shared reading, students are exposed to forms and
features they may wish to use in their own writing.

There are many reasons for using shared reading to examine a text model, for
example, to identify the form, to explore the writer's purpose for choosing that
form, to identify how the form is constructed, or to consider its intended
audience. Through this kind of deliberate examination in shared reading,
teachers can help students to become more knowledgeable readers and writers.

Using published texts as models for writing

As readers of texts, students should be encouraged to think about the elements or features that make for quality in writing. Examples of rich texts can be used to study the ways in which writers use language for particular effects. Short extracts can be taken from novels, short stories, poems, or other texts and used for shared reading to develop the students' awareness and appreciation of the use of vocabulary. Poetry lends itself well to shared reading: the text is often short enough to transcribe onto chart paper or overhead transparencies, and repeated readings can move the focus from enjoying a poem to studying the writer's use of vocabulary. Journals, letters, and emails provide accessible examples of personal writing.

In the following example the teacher used a text that was familiar to her students.

Personal writing

When Melanie first shared the story *Postcards* (Paris, 2002), her students were able to identify and relate to the form and purpose of writing used in postcards. The story was made up of a series of postcards sent by a father and son on vacation. The postcards showed two different points of view about the vacation. The objective of her second lesson with the same text was to identify the writer's purpose. In the course of the discussion, Melanie was able to guide the students to identify that the writer's purpose was probably to amuse by showing the reader that characters in a story can have different points of view. Melanie asked her students to debate the appropriateness of the form (postcards) to this purpose.

After further discussion about the form of writing needed in a postcard, the students went on to write their own postcard stories in pairs, identifying the activities that some had enjoyed and others had not at a recent school camp.

Angelsea Tuesday.

Dear Ellen,

We went on a 60 foot swing today. It was terrifying. I didn't go to the top. When I got off I realised I hated it.

From Tess

Ellen Waters
A.V.P.S Bank St
Ascot Vale 3032

By emphasizing the forms of texts and the purposes and audiences for which they are written, teachers can deepen their students' understanding and help them to ask more thoughtful questions as they meet new kinds of texts. Teachers also provide access to models of forms that students can try out in their own writing.

When selecting text for a shared reading lesson that will be followed by a writing exercise, it is important to identify one specific purpose for the discussion and to explain the purpose for its selection to the students. Furthermore, teachers should carefully consider what learning outcome they want the students to demonstrate. Because shared reading allows for so much versatility, the instruction must set a clear purpose for each lesson. Highlighting too many features at once can result in confused students and muddled writing. When done well, shared reading not only enhances the students' ability to comprehend a variety of complex texts but provides clear models for how they can grow as writers.

Using literature as a model for writing

After reading the novel *Thief Lord* (Funke, 2000) aloud to his class, Patrick put the following short extract onto an overhead transparency to explore in a shared reading lesson. He invited the students to notice the way the writer conveyed the feeling of a crisp fall day.

> It was autumn in Venice when Victor first heard of Prosper and Bo. The canals, gleaming in the sun, dappled the ancient brickwork with gold. But the wind was blowing ice-cold air from the sea, reminding the Venetians that winter was approaching. Even the air in the alleyways tasted of snow, and only the wings of the carved angels and dragons high up on the rooftops felt any real warmth from the pale sun.
>
> from *Thief Lord* by Cornelia Funke, 2000, page 7

Patrick used the following prompts:

- *This is the first paragraph of the novel. How does the writer use it to create a sense of place and time?*
- *What mood does it convey?*
- *How does she use descriptive language to create sensory images?*
- *How does she use contrast? To what effect?*
- *How does she create a sense of anticipation? Why is that important?*

Patrick's questions, and others like them, can be used effectively in shared reading. By using many different pieces of writing to examine writers' purposes and analyze the features of effective or quality writing, teachers can show students how to widen their own writing repertoire.

Using student writing as models

As well as using published texts for shared reading, teachers can use examples of student work. Pieces that show the progression or development of a student writer's idea from first draft to publication can also act as a model for refining and editing. Using student writing for shared reading is a dramatic way to help students analyze their own writing or motivate them to try something new.

This public use of student writing must always be done with extreme care. Students must give permission for their work to be used in this way, and the work must always be treated with respect by their classmates. It may be better in some situations to share writing samples with other teachers and delete names to avoid any risk of embarrassment to the writer.

The following explanation was written by Lewis, a seventh grade student, in the course of a five-week study of expository writing. The teacher had used many different instructional strategies, and this piece was based on discussion and investigation of the body parts used in speaking. The version reproduced in the example is Lewis's second draft. The teacher used it (with Lewis's permission) in a shared reading lesson to demonstrate the process that lead up to the draft and to engage the class in discussion about ways that they could improve their own writing. Some of the teacher's specific questions about the writing are shown.

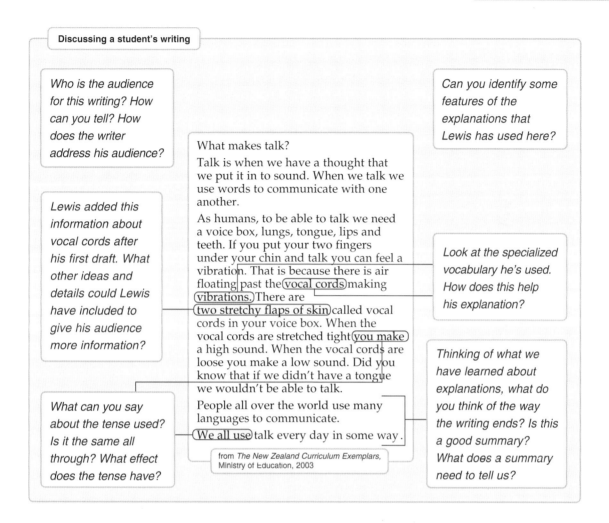

Discussing a student's writing

Who is the audience for this writing? How can you tell? How does the writer address his audience?

Lewis added this information about vocal cords after his first draft. What other ideas and details could Lewis have included to give his audience more information?

What can you say about the tense used? Is it the same all through? What effect does the tense have?

What makes talk?

Talk is when we have a thought that we put it in to sound. When we talk we use words to communicate with one another.

As humans, to be able to talk we need a voice box, lungs, tongue, lips and teeth. If you put your two fingers under your chin and talk you can feel a vibration. That is because there is air floating past the vocal cords making vibrations. There are two stretchy flaps of skin called vocal cords in your voice box. When the vocal cords are stretched tight you make a high sound. When the vocal cords are loose you make a low sound. Did you know that if we didn't have a tongue we wouldn't be able to talk.

People all over the world use many languages to communicate. We all use talk every day in some way.

from *The New Zealand Curriculum Exemplars,*
Ministry of Education, 2003

Can you identify some features of the explanations that Lewis has used here?

Look at the specialized vocabulary he's used. How does this help his explanation?

Thinking of what we have learned about explanations, what do you think of the way the writing ends? Is this a good summary? What does a summary need to tell us?

From text models to shared writing

In the next example, a class of eight year olds was studying poetry as a form of writing. This study took several days and involved sharing many kinds of poems, such as rhymed poetry, free verse, haiku, and the acrostic. Although these students happened to be in third grade, the same lesson could be adapted and delivered at all age levels. The students were exposed to many different styles by different writers, and shared reading was an excellent way for the whole class not only to enjoy the lyric quality of poetry but to analyze the writer's craft. The objective of this particular lesson was to identify expressive language in poetry and then explore how to use it in writing. The teacher followed the shared reading with shared writing by brainstorming and collaboratively writing a poem on the whiteboard.

Using text models

Rachel chose *Write a Poem* because it was a good example of a particular form. It contained a repeating phrase that students could use as an anchor in their own composition, and it skillfully demonstrated the use of expressive language to "show, not tell."

Shared reading

Using an enlarged version of the poem, Rachel asked her class: "What features can we identify that helped the writer make this poem come to life?" The list of features, generated by the students but guided by Rachel's careful questioning, included alliteration, onomatopoeia, repeating phrases, and "action language." The students did not have the names for these poetic devices but could identify, for instance, that many words started with the same letter. Rachel was then able to build on their observation by using the teachable moment. When Rachel introduced the word "alliteration," the students immediately wanted to add it to the "new word" list in the classroom!

Write a Poem

Write a poem –
make it whistle,
make it whisper,
make it whirl.

Write a poem –
make it happy,
make it hiss,
make it howl.

Write a poem –
make it spooky,
make it squirm,
make it squawl.

Write a poem –
make it yodel,
make it yelp,
make it YOURS!!!

Desna Wallace, 2002

---

amazing
amusing
affectional
appetising
advertuous
abominable
angry
accessible

Inportant
Imaginary
Immortal
Immortal
Incredible
Incredulous
interesting
Impossible
Incorrigible
Indigenous

ours
objectionable
outragous
ordinary

Scowl
Shake
Spin
Swirl
Scary
Swift
Sharp
Simple
Simple
Spooky

Next, Rachel asked the students to use a buddy, a dictionary, or a thesaurus to help them brainstorm a list of alliterative words. She challenged them to choose a letter other than the ones employed by the writer and to find some "big, juicy" words they could use in their poem.

Shared writing

Together, Rachel and the students rewrote the first two verses of the poem as a shared writing exercise on the whiteboard. Each student copied these verses into their writing notebooks. When she was sure that everyone understood how to continue, Rachel asked the students to each rewrite the next two verses themselves using the words from the lists they had brainstormed. She reminded them to use the class-created verses as well as the original poem as models. She added the challenge to end the poem with the line "make it your OWN!!!"

By combining shared reading and shared writing, Rachel was able to provide the level of support needed to launch her students into their own independent writing. In this way, they learned to use the original poem's structure as a guide and a model. By scribing on the whiteboard for the first two verses as the students gave their ideas, Rachel was able to scaffold the creative process for her students. She used the "think aloud" technique to show how writers make decisions about words and images as they work. The ideas that the students contributed were savored, discussed, considered, and combined so that everyone's voice was honored. When disagreements occurred about what should be included in the collaborative poem, Rachel guided them towards consensus and also modeled how to make editorial decisions while crafting a piece of writing. Not all the ideas could be included, so she showed them how to try out and then discard phrases that didn't sound right.

All the students were able to take the model and develop it further in subsequent writing sessions. Rachel created a checklist of features for the students to keep and refer to as they went on to write further poems independently. Through the process of shared reading, Rachel's class learned how to identify the unique features of a form of poetry, expand their own poetic vocabulary, and increase their ability to write quality poems of their own.

> Write a poem
>
> Write a poem-
> Make it astonishing,
> make it amazing,
> make it adventurous.
>
> Write a poem-
> make it Imaginary,
> make it Intelligent,
> make it Incredulous.
>
> Write a poem-
> Make it simple,
> make it sharp,
> make it scowl.
>
> Write a poem-
> make it outrageous,
> make it ordinary,
> make it ours!
>
> by Isabelle

In the example above, shared writing allowed the students to feel comfortable and supported as they wrote poetry. For those students challenged by the task, particularly English language learners, the shared writing process enabled them to feel a part of the process, and to feel that they were on an equal footing with their fellow students and with the writer.

Discussing and working together to develop a piece of writing helps all the students in the group to feel ownership and build confidence for future endeavors. Even the most reluctant writers can have a voice and contribute to creating the final product. Shared reading and shared writing complement and reinforce each other in a natural way, which further strengthens the reciprocal relationship between reading and writing in the minds of the students.

Modeling or copying?

Shared reading is an excellent technique for examining the difference between using a guide to improve one's own writing and copying someone else's words. It is essential to make students aware of this distinction and to help them become wary of plagiarism (passing another writer's work off as your own). This awareness is particularly important because students are required to use reference materials when writing for social studies and other content areas. Too frequently, students use reference material by simply copying sentences or whole chunks of writing from another text (encyclopedias, textbooks, the Internet) without any attempt to process the ideas. Students using this form of "research" learn little about the topic especially when the teacher accepts their work as meeting the task requirements.

For some students, especially English language learners and reluctant writers unfamiliar with a genre, first attempts at using a model for writing may indeed be direct copies. Because writing is a developmental process, some students may need to use a sample of someone else's writing in order to experience success. Teachers will find that repeatedly modeling "how to put it in your own words," helps students to develop an understanding of how to attempt more original writing. Modeling writing on that of others is a standard and accepted way for students to improve and expand their own writing ability, but it is the teacher's job to guide them toward independence and originality.

Detractors of this process may believe that it leads to students simply regurgitating the model, but this has not been our experience. In applying this model, teachers see themselves as the providers of rich and varied texts and the students as experts on their lives. It's the teacher's job to bring the two together so that students can write powerfully, with clarity of thought and beauty of expression, on topics that are real and important to them.

Jayne Jackson, deputy principal, in Ministry of Education, 2002, page 10

Writing in response to literature

The shared reading process results in rich conversations between the students and the teacher. These discussions may encourage a thoughtful and personal response to a text or invite a more critical evaluation of a piece. By encouraging students to read closely and look further into literary texts of all kinds, teachers can extend students' vocabularies, increase their understanding of the effects of words, language features, and techniques, and help them to think critically about language and meaning. Such understanding will enhance and enrich students' writing as they respond to the texts they have read.

Responding in writing to a text can be based on a few guiding questions. These questions need to relate to the kind of text, the teaching objectives, and the experience of the students. Some suggestions include:

- *What do you think this text is about?*
- *Why do you think it was written and for whom?*
- *What is your reaction to it?*
- *What personal connections do you have with the text?*
- *Do you understand, agree with, or like what it is saying?*
- *What devices or features has the writer used? What purpose do they serve? Are they effective?*
- *How can you support what you think about this text?*

Students often need support and guidance on how to organize their thoughts into writing as a response to reading. The use of graphic organizers, writing frames, and other templates can be powerful tools for helping the teacher capture the thoughts and ideas generated in a shared reading discussion. These tools are discussed in more detail on pages 36–37. Examples of published reviews of books, films, and television shows can also be used in shared reading to further emphasize the different ways in which people can respond to the work of others.

Responding to literature

When Sandi read the poem *Comfortable Old Chair* (Kuskin, 1992) with her class in a shared reading lesson, her first purpose was to elicit a personal response to the poem. She asked her students what they thought about the poem, whether they liked it, and whether it had any relevance for them. Her students were enthusiastic and identified with the poet's thoughts about having a safe place to dream. She was surprised at how many students said that they had a special place at home where they liked to curl up and read. Sandi then spent time working carefully through the poem with the class, asking them to be more specific about their responses. Responses included:

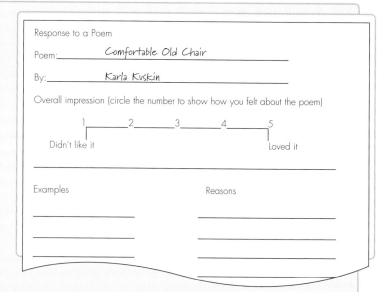

I know what those things are, so it makes me feel comfortable just reading about them.

It's nice to read about someone else's special place.

I like it when she says "to scheme a few outlandish schemes." I like the sound of those words. It's a bit like when you think about doing crazy things, but you don't really do them.

She also helped her students identify the poet's use of comparisons ("A bird has a nest ...") and descriptive language ("Soft pillowed blue ...") as features that they especially liked.

In a second lesson, she again read the poem aloud. Several students joined in the reading, obviously enjoying the words and the rhythms of the poem. This time, Sandi wanted her students to put their responses on paper. This was an activity many students found difficult, so she used a writing frame she had drawn up herself on chart paper to help them organize their thinking. She asked them to circle a number on a scale to indicate their overall impression. She then helped them identify exactly what it was about the poem that they enjoyed or disliked, finding examples in the poem and giving reasons for choosing them.

When the writing frame was partly completed, Sandi invited any students who felt they were ready to write a response on their own to move quietly to their desks. She continued to work with the students on the rug. Soon everyone had the confidence and understanding to take a blank copy of the writing frame and complete it on their own.

Writing to demonstrate understanding

When students produce an original piece of writing based on a text model from shared reading, they are demonstrating their understanding of how that text functions. They can also demonstrate their knowledge of the form and show their understanding of its unique features. The writing that follows shared reading can help teachers produce evidence for assessment purposes and can give them information for evaluating their own teaching. For example, the writing produced as a result of shared reading can be a valid exercise in responding to text and a means by which the teacher can evaluate the quality of the students' writing, the depth of their understanding, or their ability to write in different styles. There are of course limitations to this: many students understand far more than they are able to record in writing.

In the following example, a fourth grade class was studying World War II as a social studies topic.

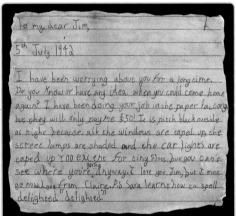

Demonstrating knowledge

Joseph, a grade 4 teacher, found a novel to use in a unit study of World War II. The novel was based on fact and had many colorful descriptions of what life was like for children in England during the war. Joseph read the book aloud to the class over several days. Then he isolated some key parts of the text and enlarged them for shared reading. He encouraged the students to use clues from the text and illustrations to help them think about what life might have been like if they had been living in England in the early 1940s. Joseph's objective for this lesson was to develop the students' use of an authentic voice in their writing. He wanted his students to "put themselves in the shoes" of another person in order to imagine their thoughts, feelings, and inner voice. In addition, Joseph wanted to find out what they had learned about World War II during the unit study.

To address his objective, Joseph had his students each craft a letter. He wanted them to write from outside their own experience, relying closely on what they had learned from their World War II study. In particular, he used selected extracts from the novel in a shared reading lesson to focus their attention on the personal experiences of the characters. He asked the students to imagine they lived in the 1940s and to write a letter describing their lives to a soldier away at the war. Joseph then used these same pieces of writing for part of his evaluation of the unit. He knew that the writing produced would be a partial indicator of how much the students had learned about life during World War II.

Using graphic organizers, templates, and writing frames

News Report

What?	Who?	When?	Why?	How?

Headline: _____

Byline: _____

Introduction: _____
_____

Quotations from: _____ _____ _____
Photographs of: _____ _____ _____
Captions: _____ _____ _____

These tools can help students to organize and plan their thoughts and ideas during the shared reading lesson and before writing. Used in conjunction with shared reading, writing frames can be used alongside the shared text as the teacher guides students to move from reading to writing. Again the emphasis needs to be on the process rather than the product. Students need to see why these tools are useful and how they can help them to become better writers and readers. For reluctant writers, writing frames also help to break up the daunting task of filling a large, blank page. For more information, see pages 36–37.

Across the curriculum

Teachers at all levels and in all areas of the curriculum will find many opportunities to make links between reading, writing, listening, and speaking. Shared reading engages students in three of those language processes. This chapter has shown some of the ways that shared reading can be used to help students learn about, engage in, and develop their skills in writing.

CHAPTER 11

Launching a Shared Reading Program

This chapter is addressed directly to teachers. It covers many of the practical considerations, logistical details, and questions of implementation that teachers may have when launching a shared reading program.

Where does everyone sit?

To avoid management challenges in the future, it is worth investing the time in classroom setup. First, all the students need to see the text without straining or leaning. It's their job to construct meaning from the text. Therefore, it's the teacher's job to make sure the text is visually accessible. (Don't give them an excuse to "check out" because they can't see!) Secondly, an intimate gathering is much more conducive to the kinds of discussion and collaborative work teachers are trying to facilitate through shared reading.

How can I create a meeting area when I have no budget and no space?

You can create a meeting area by simply rearranging the desks or tables. The size of the room and the number of desks do of course affect the amount of meeting space, but even a small area can be used. Here are some possibilities:

- Acquire a suitable-sized rug to become the designated meeting area. Carpet stores may sell or donate carpet squares, samples, or seconds for this purpose.

- Construct, with help from parents or students, bench seating that can form the outer boundaries of the meeting area. Sturdy plastic crates can be used, with planks laid across them and fastened securely. These benches can double as shelf space if they are made with the crates on their sides.

- Arrange the classroom so that there is a central space that the students can move to quickly and quietly.

But my kids are too big to sit on the rug!

In primary classes, it is perfectly natural for the teacher to gather the class together on the floor for meetings, for lessons, to enjoy a book together, or to celebrate achievements. Many primary classrooms are fitted with carpets or rugs. Teachers and parents may supply cushions or beanbags, and some rooms even have couches and comfortable chairs to facilitate a cozy, homey atmosphere in the classroom. The value of this intimate setting shouldn't be reserved only for the youngest students. Take the risk and give it a try. You'll be surprised at how changing the physical space can yield great dividends.

Some teachers find the idea of their students sitting on the floor undignified or potentially disruptive. Some students may feel they are too old to gather around their teacher "like little kids." But many teachers who value the concept of the class as a community have found ways of gathering their older students together in ways that everyone finds comfortable and supportive. The new arrangements are also conducive to good learning and community building within the class. Consider visiting another teacher's classroom to find effective models of classroom layouts. This kind of exchange and research usually achieves a lot more than the ideas alone. It can build collaborative relationships among teachers and enhance professional learning.

How can my students move to the meeting area without fuss?

Once you've arranged the seating, work on developing an efficient routine for coming together in the meeting area. Decide on the signal to be used and practice it with the class or with groups until the transition becomes fast and quiet. Teachers often report having difficulty with such transitions, especially when they are asking everyone to move at once. It is worth discussing methods with your colleagues: this is one of those areas of a teacher's life than can cause a great deal of frustration yet is rarely discussed openly. Try to arrange a staff meeting to share the methods teachers use. You will find that a lot of very simple techniques can be learned from other teachers. Some suggestions are listed here:

- Use a simple, clear verbal command in a neutral voice repeated no more than once, for example, "Everyone to the meeting area now, please."

- Ring a bell, very sparingly, to signal a change of activity. This works well in schools where students are accustomed to bells that signal a change of class, recess, lunch, or the end of the school day.

- Use one clap of your hands or a clapping pattern. This may be considered too juvenile with older students.

- Turn the overhead lights off and on.

- Move the class group by group to avoid the noise of thirty-five seats scraping at the same time.

Whatever approach you use, it's important to create some ceremony around the shared reading process. Students will respond with respect and maturity if a tone of seriousness is established from the beginning. Invest some time initially to setting high expectations and creating a culture of mutual respect. The more regular and predictable the routine, the less disruptive the transition will be.

What kinds of tools do I need for my shared reading program?

An overhead projector

An overhead projector is standard issue in many classrooms, especially in middle and high schools. If not, librarians, media centers, and veteran teachers often have under-utilized projectors stashed away. If necessary, ask for help locating one. Overhead projectors allow you to be truly creative in selecting texts.

> Warning: making copies of copyright materials without permission may be illegal. Check with the publisher, local authorities, or copyright holder to find out whether you can reproduce the material for teaching purposes.

You will need to know where to find spare bulbs and how to keep the projector in good order. It's essential to find or purchase a table of the right height to be able to project straight ahead. It is not a good idea to project upwards from the floor or a low table. The image is distorted, making reading unnecessarily difficult. When you set up your classroom at the start of the school year, take the position of the overhead projector into account. Seating and safety need to be considered as well as visibility and lighting. All this requires initial planning and time but helps to ensure the success of the lessons and increases the students' involvement.

Screens

A pull-down screen is ideal because it can be put away when you're not using it. These screens are usually designed to minimize reflection. If your classroom does not have a purpose-built screen, there are other options:

- Pull-down maps can become screens if they are turned around or (if the map is out of date) painted over in a flexible, non-reflective white paint. You may need permission to do this.

- Plain white plastic tablecloth fabric, sold by the yard at craft or hardware stores, can be pinned on a wall as a screen.

- Dry-erase whiteboards, either permanently attached to the wall or free-standing, can be used as a screen, but the reflection needs to be checked. If the text cannot be read easily from all angles, the lighting in the room will need to be altered or a different surface used.

- One or more large sheets of matt white paper or thin card can be pinned on the wall or propped on an easel to create a screen. Once again, the teacher needs to check that the resulting image is clear from every seating position.

Transparencies

Some publishers produce overhead transparencies for use in shared reading. Many are excellent and beautifully illustrated, but the text density must always be checked before they are used. If the text is too closely printed, it will be difficult to read and unsuitable for shared reading.

You can easily make your own transparencies by using a photocopier and the right kind of acetate. You can place the same kind of transparency sheets over the text transparency and write on them with wipeable marker pens to demonstrate specific points on the text. You can mask parts of the text by blacking them out on the clear overlay or by applying thin strips of paper or adhesive notes. A clear overlay also allows the text transparency to be used many times. An inexpensive idea is to put the transparency into a clear ring binder pocket. This keeps the transparency clean and easily accessible for a later session.

Finally, the print size must be large enough to be read when projected. When typing texts, use a large font and double-spacing. The amount of text on the page should be limited. Check the transparencies for readability from a distance before using them with a large group.

Using and making enlarged texts

Some excellent big books and enlarged-print posters are available that have been designed especially for older students. If your school has a photocopier that enlarges text, experiment producing clear, very large copies of texts. You will probably need to do this in stages – enlarging parts of the text, then piecing them together. Enlarging a standard letter-sized page to double size will not be big enough for a group of more than five or six students to see. Using a large font size when writing texts on the computer makes this enlargement process easier.

Many schools have a chart maker, which produces a poster-sized copy from a letter-sized sheet. A chart maker is a wonderful resource because you can use and mark up the posters and then display them in the classroom as models for the students to refer to in their future learning. Like transparencies, if stored carefully, these posters can be used many times.

Pocket charts and sentence strips are good for creating resources for shared reading: poetry, quotes, first drafts, student work, and excerpts from texts can be written out on the sentence strips. You or the students can then "edit" the text by cutting the strips apart, reordering them, or adding in new ideas. They could also be used to show students how to deconstruct complex sentences.

Blank big books are available that can have text written in them for use in shared reading. The writing can be done by yourself or by a student with clear, tidy printing. The books can also be used for shared or interactive writing. Groups of students may like to write their own big book for class sharing. The key to any hand-written text is clarity: the print must be clearly visible to everyone in the group – and, of course, the spelling, grammar, and punctuation should be correct if the text is to be used as an example.

Teacher-made enlarged texts are probably one of the oldest kinds of teaching aid. All experienced teachers have made posters, charts, books, and other forms of text for different purposes. If you are new to making teaching resources, here are a few suggestions:

- Plan out the writing before putting pen to paper.

- Use a pencil and ruler to mark lines, and then draft the word placement – nothing is more frustrating than coming to the last two lines of a poem with no room to write them.

- Spread the text out over two or more pages rather than have it so cramped that it cannot be easily read across the room.

- Using markers that give a relatively thick line, write in best schoolteacher printing rather than cursive script. The aim is readability, not modeling handwriting.

- Check and double-check spelling and grammar because what teachers do themselves is always a model for their students.

An easel, preferably with a lower ledge as well as a top rail with binder clips, is useful for holding big books, posters, and charts.

Storage

Big books, posters, and charts pose storage problems in most busy classrooms. Solutions range from specially designed storage drawers, shelves, and cabinets to clothes racks with clip hangers. A clothesline and clothespins can be used to display enlarged texts and student work or can provide additional storage out of the way. It is useful to talk to primary teachers to find out what they use and to share ideas.

Accessories

Chart paper or whiteboards

Chart paper and a dry-erase whiteboard of similar size are invaluable aids to a shared reading lesson. Appropriate markers or pens are also needed as well as an eraser for the whiteboard. Poster-sized pads of chart paper with a sticky strip at the top are available commercially. They are like giant adhesive notes and can be

easily displayed on the walls after use. During shared reading lessons, this
equipment is needed for many purposes such as:

- to record students' predictions, observations, or responses;

- to note words that should be followed up in a word study lesson;

- to demonstrate the use of a strategy;

- to break down words into their component parts;

- to write a sentence to demonstrate features of grammar;

- to create a graphic organizer to clarify thinking;

- to make a diagram to show relationships within a story;

- to generate lists of synonyms;

- to brainstorm ideas or associations about words.

You may want your students to share these tasks to engage in shared or
interactive writing, so the teaching aids should be easily accessible to students.
Such participation encourages and heightens active engagement. Charts created
in this way can be displayed in the classroom for reference for later group or
independent work or can be used as examples of shared writing. Charts can be
stored by laminating them and clipping them onto trouser hangers so that they
can be hung from a hook or rack.

Sticky things
Adhesive notes of various sizes are useful during shared reading. Some examples
of their use are:

- to demonstrate and model note making;

- to write labels and captions;

- to record questions raised during the reading;

- to record predictions, observations, and responses;

- to highlight specific features, such as main ideas, foreshadowing of events, or
  chronological order.

Transparent, colored highlighter tape can be used for drawing attention to
particular words or other features.

Many other materials can be used in novel ways to help you achieve your
purposes in shared reading, but the bottom line must always be the visibility
and clarity of the text for all students. There is a danger of trying to do too

many different things in one lesson. For example, a teacher who used different colored pens to circle parts of the text for three different purposes had an unreadable text and very confused students by the end of the lesson. If a shared reading text finishes the lesson looking like a college dorm notice board, you have probably gone too far! What is done to the text should be explicitly linked to the objectives of the lesson.

Pointers

The reason for using a pointer is to help focus the students' attention on the text. In primary grades, teachers use pointers to indicate the features of the print, such as the beginnings of words, the places to start reading, or the return sweep at the end of each line. Students in upper grades may not require this level of attention to letters and to print conventions. However, they may well benefit from support in identifying more advanced text features, such as grammatical constructions, patterns in poetry, and nonfiction features (like labels on diagrams, flow charts, and maps). A pointer needs to be long enough for you to use without your arm covering any of the text but fine enough not to obscure the text itself. A long chopstick, a wooden knitting pin, or a length of thin dowel are all suitable. Pens with an extendable "aerial" are ideal and readily available. Most rulers are too wide to be suitable as pointers.

If you're using an overhead projector, practice using a fine pen or pencil on the projector as a pointer. Trying to point to the projected text on the screen itself is not a good idea because it usually means having to stand between the text and the students and so blocking their view.

Afterword

Determining the need for reading instruction: a staff development activity

Most young children learn to read through narrative fiction. They are therefore not as familiar with the structure and vocabulary of nonfiction. According to research, students in the early years only spend an average of 3.6 minutes a day exploring nonfiction texts (Duke, 2000). However, as students move through the grades in elementary school, the demands on them to read complex informational text increase dramatically. As a result, many students experience what is often referred to as the "fourth grade slump" when their confidence and achievement suffer in the face of these new challenges. This struggle continues for many students throughout middle and high school and is reflected in lower test scores.

Without explicit instruction on the skills and strategies to use when encountering informational text, many students never catch up. This achievement gap is often widened when teachers in middle and high school assume that their students are competent nonfiction readers. They see their job as teaching content to students. Students' success in these classes depends on their reading and understanding a large volume of information in textbooks.

The following activity[1] has been designed to help teachers reflect on the reading challenges that their students face on a daily basis. It asks teachers to look at all the reading materials a typical student might face (fiction and nonfiction). It can be used as an opportunity for staff development at one or across several grade levels.

Assessing the reading demands that students face

Arrange for a meeting to discuss reading materials with all the teachers and other adults that any typical student in a specific class would encounter in an average school week. Include the teachers of all specials (such as physical education, music, computers, art, library, and second language instruction) and other school support staff (such as counselors, cafeteria workers, speech

[1] Adapted from an idea developed by Melanie Winthrop, literacy consultant, with permission.

teachers, and reading specialists). Ask them to bring with them all the texts or environmental print the student may have to read or is expected to use in one week. Ask them to reproduce or gather all of this reading material including "incidental" items, such as computer menus, websites, instructions, and notes. Lay the texts out on a table. This collection could include:

- a poem;

- a class novel;

- an independent reading book;

- a newspaper article;

- several worksheets;

- pages in a math textbook;

- math problems;

- instructions for a class project;

- social studies source books;

- a science textbook;

- texts that contain maps, graphs, charts, and diagrams;

- a school notice.

This activity will demonstrate the great variety of texts that a typical student may be faced with each day or week. Discuss which materials are new to the student and where the reading takes place. Can the student actually read these texts? Is any instructional scaffolding provided? Is the setting noisy or distracting? How much processing time is given? How is the student expected to respond? What are the parental expectations for this student? What support does the student's home provide? All these factors influence the reading transaction.

For many teachers, this activity will be an eye-opening experience. If you or your colleagues feel overwhelmed by the challenges uncovered by this activity, you can initiate a discussion about the variety of texts and reading expectations the students in a particular grade may face. From this initial exploration, you can consider one particular student of concern, a group of students, or one aspect of the curriculum.

Think about how shared reading can help to address some of these reading challenges. Remember, shared reading can take a variety of forms, and the "expert reader" who does the modeling and scaffolding doesn't always have to be the teacher.

Some prompts to help facilitate this reflective investigation might include:

- *How many students in your classes have the reading skills necessary to understand the material given to them?*
- *Whose job is it to teach these skills? How can they best be taught?*
- *Can these skills or strategies be reinforced in all the classes?*
- *What can our students already do? How will this help us to teach them new reading skills?*
- *What instructional techniques or approaches do your colleagues use that could be adapted for your class?*
- *How can we provide more appropriate texts?*
- *How do our teaching practices reflect our curriculum objectives?*
- *What impact does this have on our school planning?*

Taken over a whole class or grade level, it may become obvious that some (possibly many) students will be missing out if they don't have the reading skills demanded by such an array of texts.

Shared reading is an easy approach for all teachers to learn and use. If teachers across the curriculum were to come together to examine the texts their students have to read, they could then explore the many ways that they could support their students' reading. The suggestions in this book are intended as guides to all teachers, not just those who "teach" reading.

References

Allington, R. L. (2001). *What Really Matters for Struggling Readers: Designing Research-based Programs*. New York: Addison Wesley Longman.

Allington, R. L. (2002). "Research on Reading/Learning Disability Interventions". In A. E. Farstrup and S. J. Samuels (eds), *What Research Has to Say About Reading Instruction* (3rd edition). Newark, DE: International Reading Association, pp. 261–290.

Au, K. (2002). "Multicultural Factors and the Effective Instruction of Students of Diverse Backgrounds." In A. E. Farstrup and S. J. Samuels (eds), *What Research Has to Say About Reading Instruction* (3rd edition). Newark, DE: International Reading Association, pp. 392–413.

Barell, J. (1998). Quoted in B. J. Millis and P. G. Cottell, Jr. (eds) (1998), *Cooperative Learning for the Higher Education Faculty*, Oryx Press, American Council on Education Series on Higher Education.

Baumann, J., Jones, L., and Seifert-Kessell, N. (1993). "Using Think Alouds to Enhance Children's Comprehension Monitoring Abilities." *The Reading Teacher*, vol. 47 no. 3, pp. 184–193.

Braunger, J. and Lewis, J. (1998). *Building a Knowledge Base in Reading*. Oregon: Northwest Regional Educational Laboratory's Curriculum and Instruction Services.

Bruner, (1983). *Child's Talk: Learning to Use Language*. New York: Norton.

Calkins, L. (2001). *The Art of Teaching Reading*. New York: Addison-Wesley.

Clay, M. (1991). *Becoming Literate: The Construction of Inner Control*. Portsmouth, NH: Heinemann.

Daniels, H. (1994). *Literature Circles*. York, ME: Stenhouse.

Dowhower, S. (1999). "Supporting a Strategic Stance in the Classroom: A Comprehension Framework for Helping Teachers to Help Students to Be Strategic." *The Reading Teacher*, vol. 52 no. 7, pp. 672–683.

Duke, N. (2002). "Informational Text? The Research Says, Yes!' " In L. Hoyt, M. Mooney, and B. Parkes (eds), *Exploring Informational Texts: From Theory to Practice*. Portsmouth: NH: Heinemann, pp. 2–7.

Duke, N. and Pearson, D. (2002). "Effective Practices for Developing Reading Comprehension." In A. E. Farstrup and S. J. Samuels (eds), *What Research Has to Say About Reading Instruction* (3rd edition). Newark, DE: International Reading Association, pp. 205–242.

Durkin, D. (1979). "What Classroom Observations Reveal About Reading Comprehension Instruction." *Reading Research Quarterly*, vol. 14 no. 4, pp 481–553.

Educational Department of Western Australia, (1993). *First Steps* Series. Portsmouth, NH: Heinemann.

Elley, W. (1989). "Vocabulary Acquisition from Listening to Stories." *Reading Research Quarterly*, vol. 24 no. 2, pp. 174–187.

Fountas, I. C. and Pinnell, G. S. (2001). *Guiding Readers and Writers Grades 3–6: Teaching Comprehension, Genre, and Content Literacy*. Portsmouth, NH: Heinemann.

Graves, D. (1983). *Writing: Teachers and Children at Work*. Portsmouth, NH. Heinemann.

Graves. M. and Watts-Taffe, S. (2002). "The Place of Word Consciousness in a Research-Based Vocabulary Program." In A. E. Farstrup and S. J. Samuels (eds), *What Research Has to Say About Reading Instruction* (3rd edition). Newark, DE: International Reading Association, pp. 140–165.

Harvey, S. and Goudvis, A. (2000). *Strategies That Work: Teaching Comprehension to Enhance Understanding*. York, Maine: Stenhouse Publishers.

Holdaway, D. (1979). *The Foundations of Literacy*. Portsmouth, NH: Heinemann.

Holdaway, D. (1980). *Independence in Reading*. Gosford, NSW: Ashton Scholastic.

International Association for the Evaluation of Educational Achievement, (IEA). (2000). *Framework and Specifications for PIRLS Assessment 2001*. Boston: International Study Center, Lynch School of Education, Boston College.

Johnson, D. W., Johnson, R., and Holubec, E. (1993). *Circles Of Learning*, (4th edition). Edina, MN: Interaction Book Company.

Keene, E. and Zimmermann, S. (1997). *Mosaic of Thought: Teaching Comprehension in a Reader's Workshop*. Portsmouth, NH: Heinemann.

Koskinen, P. and Blum, I., Bisson, S., Phillips, S., Creamer, T., and Baker, T. (1999). "Shared Reading Books and Audiotapes: Supporting Diverse Students in School and at Home." *The Reading Teacher*, vol. 52 no. 5, pp. 430–444.

Learning Media Limited (2000). *Steps to Guided Reading: A Professional Development Course for Grades 3 and Beyond. Course Book*. Wellington: Learning Media Limited.

Luke, A. and Freebody, P. (1997). "The Social Practice of Reading." In S. Muspratt, A. Luke, and P. Freebody (eds), *Constructing Critical Literacies*. St Leonards, NSW: Allen and Urwin.

Mercer, M. (1994). "Language in Educational Practice." In J. Bourne (ed), *Thinking Through Primary Practice*. London: Routledge.

Ministry of Education (2003). *Effective Literacy Practice*. Wellington: Learning Media Limited.

Ministry of Education (2000). *The New Zealand Curriculum Exemplars*. Wellington: Learning Media Limited.

Ministry of Education (2002). *Connections between Reading and Writing: A Professional Development Module for Schools*. Wellington: Learning Media Limited.

Mooney, M. (1988). *Developing Life-Long Learners*. Wellington. Learning Media Limited.

Moustafa, M. (1997). *Beyond Traditional Phonics. Research Discoveries and Reading Instruction*. Portsmouth, NH: Heinemann.

Opitz, M. and Rasinski, T. (1998). *Good-Bye Round Robin: 25 Effective Oral Reading Strategies*. Portsmouth: NH. Heinemann.

Oster, L. (2001). "Using the Think-aloud for Reading Instruction. *The Reading Teacher*, vol. 55 no. 1, pp. 64–69.

Palincsar, A. S. and Brown, A. L. (1985). "Reciprocal Teaching: Activities to Promote Read(ing) with Your Mind." In T. L. Harris and E. J. Cooper (eds), *Reading, Thinking and Concept Development: Strategies for the Classroom*. New York: The College Board.

Parkes, B. (2000). *Read It Again! Revisiting Shared Reading*. Portland, ME: Stenhouse Publishers.

Pearson, D. and Gallagher, M. (1983). "The Instruction of Reading Comprehension." *Contemporary Educational Psychology*, vol. 8, March 1983, pp. 317–344.

Pressley, M. and Afflerbach, P. (1995). *Verbal Protocols of Reading. The Nature of Constructively Responsive Reading*. Hillsdale, NJ: Lawrence Erlbaum.

Pressley, M. (1998). *Reading Instruction That Works: The Case for Balanced Teaching*. New York: Guilford.

Pressley, M. (2002). "A Turn-of-the-Century Status Report." In C. Collins-Block and M. Pressley (eds), *Comprehension Instruction: Research-based Best Practices*. New York: Guidford Press, pp. 11–27.

Routman, R. (2000). *Conversations: Strategies for Teaching, Learning, and Evaluating*. Portsmouth, NH: Heinemann.

Smith, J. and Elley, W. (1997). *How Children Learn to Write*. Auckland: Longman.

Swanborn, M. and de Glopper, K. (1999). "Incidental Word Learning while Reading: A Meta-analysis." *Review of Educational Research*, vol. 69 no.3, pp. 261–285.

Trabasso, T. and Bouchard, E. (2002). In C. Block and M. Pressley, (eds), *Comprehension Instruction: Research Based Best Practice*. New York: The Guilford Press, pp. 179–200.

Vacca, R. T. (2002). "Making a Difference in Adolescents' School Lives: Visible and Invisible Aspects of Content Area Reading." In A. E. Farstrup and S. J. Samuels (eds), *What Research Has To Say About Reading Instruction* (3rd edition). Newark, DE: International Reading Association, pp. 184–204.

Villaume, S. K. and Brabman, E. G. (2002). "Comprehension Instruction: Beyond Strategies." *The Reading Teacher*, vol. 55 no. 7, pp 672–675.

Vygotsky, L. S. (1978). *Mind in Society: the Development of Higher Psychological Processes*. M. Cole, V. John Steiner, S. Scribner, and E. Souberman, (eds and trans), Cambridge, MS: Harvard University Press.

Wilhelm, J. D. (2001). *Improving Comprehension with Think–Aloud Strategies*. New York. Scholastic Professional Books.

Williams, J. (2001). "Classroom Conversations: Opportunities to Learn for ESL Students in Mainstream Classrooms." *The Reading Teacher*, vol. 54 no. 8, pp. 750–757.

Worthy, J., and Broaddus, K. (2002). "Fluency beyond the Primary Grades: From Group Performance to Silent, Independent Reading." *The Reading Teacher*, vol. 55 no. 4, pp. 334–343.

References to Student Materials

Belcher, A. (2000). *Our Changing Earth*. Orbit Grade 5 Shared Reading series. Wellington: Learning Media Limited.

Bennett, J. (2002). *Follow the Flow*. New Heights series. Wellington: Learning Media Limited.

Bishop, N. (2003). *Animal Neighbors*. Orbit Grade 4 Double Takes series. Wellington: Learning Media Limited.

Bonallack, J. (2000). *Finding Your Way*. Orbit Grade 5 Chapter Books series. Wellington: Learning Media Limited.

Bornholdt, J. (2002). "City Song." In *It's Our World*. Orbit Grade 4 Collections series. Wellington: Learning Media Limited.

Bornholdt, J. (2004). "Twister." In *The Voice of the Glacier and Other Poems*. Orbit Grade 5 Double Takes series. Wellington: Learning Media Limited.

Crum, A. (2003). *The Great and Shining Road*. Orbit Grade 5 Chapter Books series. Wellington: Learning Media Limited.

Duder, T. (2001). *Restoring Tissot*. Applications series. Wellington: Learning Media Limited.

Duksta, C. (2000). *Twisting Up a Storm*. Orbit Grade 4 Chapter Books series. Wellington: Learning Media Limited.

Frances, H. (2002). "Home-made Movie Makeup." In *School Journal*, Part 3, Number 2, 2002. Wellington: Learning Media Limited.

Funke, C. (2002). *The Thief Lord*. Somerset: The Chicken House.

Griff, P. (2000). *Nory Ryan's Song*. New York: Delacorte Press.

Hill, S. (2001). "Should Mac Leave Town?" In *I Say, You Say*. Orbit Grade 3 Collections series. Wellington: Learning Media Limited.

Hill, S. (2003). *Lost in the Dark*. Orbit Grade 4 Double Takes series. Wellington: Learning Media Limited.

Kenna, A. (1999). *How I Met Archie*. Orbit Grade 4 Chapter Books series. Wellington: Learning Media Limited.

Kuskin, K. (1992) "Comfortable Old Chair." In M. Rosen (ed). *Home: A Collaboration of Thirty Distinguished Authors and Illustrators of Children's Books to Aid the Homeless*. New York: HarperCollins Publishers.

Lang, R. (2002). *The Statue of Liberty*. New Heights series. Wellington: Learning Media Limited.

Lasenby, J. (1999). *The Shaman and the Droll*. Dunedin: Longacre Press.

Learning Media Limited. (2001). "Kids Inc." in *Eureka!* Orbit Grade 3 Collections series. Wellington: Learning Media Limited.

Learning Media Limited. (2004). *Global Warming*. Orbit Grade 6 Shared Reading series. Wellington: Learning Media Limited.

Leunig, M. (1982). *There's No Place Like Home*. Victoria: Penguin.

Lockyer, J. (2002). *Looking at Letters*. Orbit Grade 3 Double Takes series. Wellington: Learning Media Limited.

Mahuika, K. (1997). *In the Dark Forest*. Learning Media Literacy series. Wellington: Learning Media Limited.

Morris, R. (2000). *Tasmanian Devils*. Orbit Grade 4 Shared Reading series. Wellington: Learning Media Limited.

O'Brien, B. (2002). *Animals in Danger*. Orbit Grade 3 Double Takes series. Wellington: Learning Media Limited.

Paris, S. (2002). "Postcards." In *Going Places*. Orbit Grade 4 Collections. Wellington: Learning Media Limited.

Sachar, L. (1998). *Holes*. New York: Farrar, Straus and Giroux, LLC.

Schoof, H. (2003). *Helen Keller: A Life of Adventure*. Orbit Grade 3 Chapter Books series. Huntington Beach, CA: Pacific Learning.

Slack, P. (2002). *Picasso*. New Heights series. Wellington: Learning Media Limited

Spinelli, J. (1997). *Wringer*. London: Collins.

Taylor, W. (2000). *Scarface and the Angel*. Dunedin: Longacre Press.

Thomson, J. (2000). "From Rock to Rock." In *Connected 3*. Wellington: Learning Media Limited.

Time Inc. (2003). *Time for Kids* vol. 9 no. 2. New York: Time Inc.

Tuwhare, H. (1964). "Rain." In *No Ordinary Sun*. Auckland: Blackwood and Janet Paul.

Wallace, D. (2001). "Write a Poem." In *School Journal*, Part 2, Number 2, 2002. Wellington: Learning Media Limited.

Wilson, A. (1994). "New House." In *Peaches: Secondary Students' Writing*. Wellington: Learning Media Limited for the Ministry of Education.

www.orbitforkids.com

www.yahooligans.com

Young, J. (2002). "On the Road in Sudan." In *Going Places*. Orbit Grade 4 Collections. Wellington: Learning Media Limited.

Zindel, P. (1968). *The Pigman*. Glasgow: William Collins Sons and Co Ltd.

Index